Wacky Science

Fun and Exciting Hands-On Activities for the Classroom

Phil Parratore
Illustrated by Ellen Connor

PRUFROCK PRESS INC.
WACO, TEXAS

Library of Congress Cataloging-in-Publication Data

Parratore, Phil.
Wacky science : fun and exciting hands-on activities for the classroom / Phil Parratore.
    p. cm.
  ISBN 978-1-59363-411-7 (pbk.)
  1. Science--Study and teaching--Activity programs. I. Title.
  LB1585.P38 2010
  507.1--dc22
                              2010001608

ISBN-13: 978-1-59363-411-7
ISBN-10: 1-59363-411-0

Printed in the United States of America.

At the time of this book's publication, all facts and figures cited are the most current available. All telephone numbers, addresses, and website URLs are accurate and active. All publications, organizations, websites, and other resources exist as described in the book, and all have been verified. The author and Prufrock Press Inc. make no warranty or guarantee concerning the information and materials given out by organizations or content found at websites, and we are not responsible for any changes that occur after this book's publication. If you find an error, please contact Prufrock Press Inc.

Prufrock Press Inc.
P.O. Box 8813
Waco, TX 76714-8813
Phone: (800) 998-2208
Fax: (800) 240-0333
http://www.prufrock.com

Contents

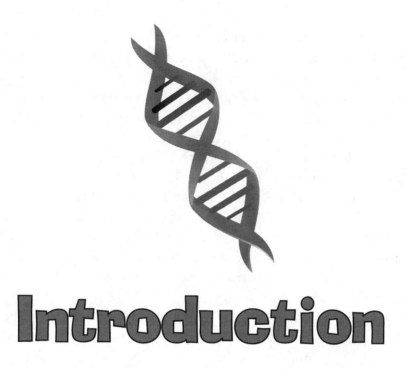

Introduction

You are about to embark on an extremely exciting adventure—an adventure of teaching hands-on science in your classroom. It is not uncommon for many teachers and parents to feel a bit intimidated when it comes to teaching hands-on science. Actually, that's perfectly normal. The challenge becomes how to overcome this fear.

Throughout our lives, we hear endless clichés such as "This is not rocket science," or "You don't have to be a brain surgeon." We often admire and place people in the science fields on a pedestal—and rightfully so. When one thinks of a scientist, the first things that come to mind are terms such as *smart, brilliant, intelligent, witty,* or *knowledgeable.* In the same vein, many educators often feel that they are unable to understand what these scientists are saying or doing.

After doing only a few of the activities in this book, you will be pleasantly surprised by how fast you have become a scientist. Even if you are comfortable teaching hands-on science, I guarantee that your current knowledge base and skills will be greatly enhanced with just a few of the activities in this book. You have the privilege of working with some of the greatest young minds on this planet. Gifted students love science, and they particularly love hands-on science. One of the most exciting things about teaching hands-on science is being able to observe how your students gravitate toward these motivating activities and their extraordinary ability to extrapolate additional scientific information from the basic concepts you are teaching them.

In this book, you'll find a variety of science experiments and informative information. Chapter 1 provides an overview of safety issues for your science classroom. In Chapter 2, you'll find a helpful student reflection form and a science scoring rubric, both of which will help you assess your students' work on the science experiments.

One of the first items you will become aware of as you start to use this book is that the "hands-on" experiments (found in Chapter 3) can be used by either you, the educator, or directly by your students. These activities give you a great deal of flexibility in your lesson plan development. Because the experiments are student-friendly, feel free to make copies and encourage your students to take home any that use common household materials (listed under the What You'll Need section). Parents of gifted students love to see their child bring entertaining and educationally stimulating hands-on science activities into their home. Encourage parents to get more involved with your hands-on science lessons by doing this on a weekly basis. Not only will you be increasing student learning, you also will be encouraging more parent involvement in your classroom. You will soon find out that parents love these types of books as much as your students.

The remaining chapters are more teacher-oriented in focus and provide lessons and additional information for you to use in your science classroom. Chapter 4, Hands-On Earth Science, provides lessons on rocks and materials designed specifically for the various learning styles found in the classroom. Chapter 5, Hands-On Overhead Projector/Document Camera Science, shares ways to use these tools to teach hands-on science. Chapters 6 and 7 offer helpful advice for spearheading science fair projects and developing high-quality field trips that enhance students' learning. Chapter 8 is a lighthearted chapter that includes fun science holiday songs.

Although I was a successful middle school math and science teacher for almost 35 years, it did take me many years to get comfortable with teaching hands-on science. My young gifted students turned out to be some of the best teachers for developing my science skills. They consistently provided me with motivation to want to learn well beyond what was in the textbook. My individual talents evolved over the years to the point that this is my 17th hands-on science resource book for educators and students. Currently, I teach university graduate courses that train teachers in the art of hands-on science. Teachers and students alike have shown me that people of all ages, backgrounds, and educational abilities love to do science that they can directly touch, hear, observe, smell, and experience.

This manual contains many high-level, abstract scientific concepts geared for students in grades 5–8, although almost all can be adapted to students of any level. This text brings the stigma of scientific complexity to a level that everyone can understand. As you proceed with the many fun, exciting, and highly motivational activities for your students, remember that you do not have to know everything about a particular topic. It is OK to say to a student, "I don't know the answer to that question. Why don't you research that and get back to me?" Just try to practice the activities in advance, relax, have fun, and know that you will be making a great impact on the lives of your students.

Chapter 1

Safety in Your Science Classroom

In your science classroom, *you* are the safety manager. You make and enforce the rules, and you set the general tone for safety procedures. This is a role you must take very seriously. A little advance preparation in your classroom will provide a safe and secure environment for you and your students. Although much has been written about science safety over the decades, in this author's opinion, the best source for science safety is Flinn Scientific, Inc. It is a well-established chemical and science supply house that caters strictly to teachers. Although there are many fine and reputable supply houses—and I have worked with most of them—I have found that Flinn Scientific, located in Batavia, IL, goes far above and beyond the basics to meet each individual teacher's needs.

The first thing you need to do is visit their website (http://www. flinnsci.com) and browse for a few minutes. If you are a certified public or private school, you can request a catalog (elementary/middle school or high school version) and get on their mailing list. An entire section of the Flinn Scientific catalog is devoted to science safety. The valuable information it provides will give you all of the details you will ever need when it comes to science safety in the classroom.

Figure 1 shows an example of a one-page teacher/student/parent contract, developed by Flinn, that summarizes all of the important variables for elementary science safety. In your own classroom, you can certainly add or subtract from them as you see fit. However, it is vital that you take the time to go through these rules with your students. It will set the tone for a safe school year in your science lab. You should develop your own safety contract, review it with your students, have them sign the contract, and then have their parent/guardian sign, as well, so students and parents alike know that you will enforce safety in your science classroom.

Flinn Scientific's Middle School Science Safety Contract

PURPOSE

Science is a hands-on laboratory class. However, science activities may have potential hazards. We will use some equipment and animals that may be dangerous if not handled properly. Safety in the science classroom is an important part of the scientific process. To ensure a safe classroom, a list of rules has been developed and is called the Science Safety Contract. These rules must be followed at all times. Additional safety instructions will be given for each activity.

No science student will be allowed to participate in science activities until this contract has been signed by both the student and a parent or guardian.

SAFETY RULES

1. Conduct yourself in a responsible manner at all times in the science room. Horseplay, practical jokes, and pranks will not be tolerated.
2. Follow all written and verbal instructions carefully. Ask your teacher questions if you do not understand the instructions.
3. Do not touch any equipment, supplies, animals, or other materials in the science room without permission from the teacher.
4. Perform only authorized and approved experiments. Do not conduct any experiments when the teacher is out of the room.
5. Never eat, drink, chew gum, or taste anything in the science room.
6. Keep hands away from face, eyes, and mouth while using science materials or when working with either chemicals or animals. Wash your hands with soap and water before leaving the science room.
7. Wear safety glasses or goggles when instructed. Never remove safety glasses or goggles during an experiment. There will be no exceptions to this rule!
8. Keep your work area and the science room neat and clean. Bring only your laboratory instructions, worksheets, and writing instruments to the work area.
9. Clean all work areas and equipment at the end of the experiment. Return all equipment clean and in working order to the proper storage area.
10. Follow your teacher's instructions to dispose of any waste materials generated in an experiment.
11. Report any accident (fire, spill, breakage, etc.), injury (cut, burn, etc.), or hazardous condition (broken equipment, etc.) to the teacher immediately.
12. Consider all chemicals used in the science room to be dangerous. Do not touch or smell any chemicals unless specifically instructed to do so.
13. Handle all animals with care and respect.
    a.-Open animal cages only with permission.
    b.-Never handle any animals when the teacher is out of the room.
    c.-Do not take animals out of the science room.
    d.-Do not tease or handle animals roughly.
    e.-Keep animals away from students' faces.
    f.-Wear gloves when handling animals.
    g.-Report any animal bite or scratch to the teacher immediately.
14. Always carry a microscope with both hands. Hold the arm with one hand; place the other hand under the base.
15. Treat all preserved specimens and dissecting supplies with care and respect.
    a.-Do not remove preserved specimens from the science room.
    b.-Use scalpels, scissors, and other sharp instruments only as instructed.
    c.-Never cut any material towards you— always cut away from your body.
    d.-Report any cut or scratch from sharp instruments to the teacher immediately.
16. Never open storage cabinets or enter the prep/storage room without permission from the teacher.
17. Do not remove chemicals, equipment, supplies, or animals from the science room without permission from the teacher.
18. Handle all glassware with care. Never pick up hot or broken glassware with your bare hands.
19. Use extreme caution when using matches, a burner, or hot plate. Only light burners when instructed and do not put anything into a flame unless specifically instructed to do so. Do not leave a lit burner unattended.
20. Dress properly—long hair must be tied back, no dangling jewelry, and no loose or baggy clothing. Wear aprons when instructed.
21. Learn where the safety equipment is located and how to use it. Know where the exits are located and what to do in case of an emergency or fire drill.

AGREEMENT

I, _____
, _____ (student's name) have read and understand each of the above safety rules set forth in this contract. I agree to follow them to ensure not only my own safety but also the safety of others in the science classroom or laboratory. I also agree to follow the general rules of appropriate behavior for a classroom at all times to avoid accidents and to provide a safe learning environment for everyone. I understand that if I do not follow all the rules and safety precautions, I will not be allowed to participate in science activities.

_____
Student Signature

_____
Date

Dear Parent or Guardian:

We feel that you should be informed of the school's effort to create and maintain a safe science classroom/laboratory environment. Please read the list of safety rules. No student will be permitted to perform science activities unless this contract is signed by both the student and parent/guardian and is on file with the teacher. Your signature on this contract indicates that you have read this Science Safety Contract, reviewed it with your child, and are aware of the measures taken to ensure the safety of your son/daughter in the science classroom.

_____
Parent/Guardian Signature

_____
Date

Important questions:
Does your child wear contact lenses?
        Y   or   N
Is your child color blind?
        Y   or   N
Does your child have any allergies?
        Y   or   N
If so, Please list:

FLINN SCIENTIFIC INC.

"Your Safer Source for Science Supplies"

P.O. Box 219, Batavia, IL 60510
1-800-452-1261 • Fax: (866) 452-1436
flinn@flinnsci.com • www.flinnsci.com

IN10642

Figure 1. Science safety contract.

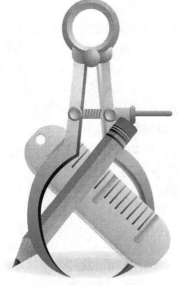

Chapter 2

Student Assessment

For gifted students, assessment of hands-on science activities can include evaluation of conceptual understanding, performance evaluation of hands-on experiments, application of knowledge, and communication of learning. Educators can assess student skills by such methods as paper-and-pencil exams, laboratory practical exams, self- and peer evaluations, learning logs, journals, conferencing, student observations, and observation checklists.

An effective, proven evaluation tool that is readily accepted by students, parents, and administrators is the rubric. A rubric is a rule or guideline that outlines the criteria and indicators of success, often being used for evaluation and scoring purposes. The indicators in a rubric, like using the scientific method, are observable, measurable behaviors that show to what degree a student is using his or her scientific knowledge and skills.

Gifted students need to have the opportunity to reflect on what they accomplished in an individual laboratory activity. Although having an open forum for discussion is a wonderful way to assess what students are thinking, it is not always feasible. Observation is a very important part of scientific inquiry. Although a rubric is an excellent evaluation tool for the teacher of gifted students, an open-ended method for students to evaluate their own progress is equally important. The best—and simplest—way to accomplish this is through a Student Reflection Form. This open-ended format allows students to not only take a careful look at what they accomplished, but to see how they can relate their learning to the real world around them. It is suggested that students use this form when the are doing activities found in Chapter 3. You should review the Student Reflection Form before the Science Scoring Rubric.

STUDENT REFLECTION FORM

Name: _____

Name of Science Activity/Experiment: _____

What did you observe in the experiment?

How do you explain what you observed in this experiment? (Use proper scientific terminology.)

How does what you learned in this science experiment connect to the things that you already know?

What questions do you have about this experiment?

SCIENCE SCORING RUBRIC

Name: _____

Name of Science Activity/Experiment: _____

Rating System: 1 = Poor   2 = Fair   3 = Good   4 = Excellent

Demonstrates understanding of scientific concepts.	1	2	3	4
Keeps accurate records of observations.	1	2	3	4
Organizes data/results through categorizing/ordering.	1	2	3	4
Draws logical conclusions from experimental results.	1	2	3	4
Effectively communicates scientific learning.	1	2	3	4
Transfers learning from one activity to another.	1	2	3	4
Relates prior knowledge to new learning.	1	2	3	4
Makes connections to science across the curriculum.	1	2	3	4
Makes inferences.	1	2	3	4
Applies knowledge to solve problems.	1	2	3	4
Uses lab equipment and supplies appropriately.	1	2	3	4
Demonstrates the scientific method.	1	2	3	4
Works cooperatively with others in lab environment.	1	2	3	4
Completes assignments/tasks on time.	1	2	3	4
Turns in work that is neatly done.	1	2	3	4

Teacher Comments:

Chapter 3

Hands-On Experiments

This chapter offers hands-on activities in the following areas:
- animal systems science,
- botany,
- entomology,
- human animal science
- paleontology,
- physics,
- and zoology.

Each section provides a brief overview of the topic and then offers experiments that focus on the science being studied. Each activity will follow the format below:
- **Purpose:** The objective of the activity.
- **Time:** Given in approximate number of minutes the experiment will take.

- **What You'll Need:** Materials needed to complete the experiment.
- **Safety/Note:** A quick caution of safety or note that may be relevant to a specific activity.
- **What to Do:** A step-by-step listing of how students are to perform each activity.
- **Explanation:** An explanation of what happened in the experiment and ties it to the topic being studied.

HANDS-ON ANIMAL SYSTEMS SCIENCE

Animals are a major group of multicellular organisms of the kingdom we call Animalia. They are the blueprint for the way the body of an organism is organized. Their individual systems eventually become fixed as they develop. Some undergo a change of form, shape, structure, or substance later on in their life. Most animals can move on impulse and without help from outside forces. Animals also can ingest other organisms for food and nutrition.

We know there are many different types of animals in the world. Many animals are quite similar to each other while others are quite different. Animals can be classified based on their similarities. Invertebrates are animals without a backbone or spinal column; vertebrates are animals with a backbone or spinal column.

So, when looking for some fun, one of the first places many people consider is a day at the zoo. Nothing brings more excitement to both adults and children than to see the roaming lions, tigers, and bear—oh, my! A trip to the zoo is a great opportunity to learn about the fascinating animals and their habitats. This section will give students a detailed look at some of the finer points about animal life and their interesting behaviors.

Lessons

Balloon Cells

Purpose: To model how groups of animal cells live together.

Time: 15 minutes

What You'll Need: fish aquarium; package of small, round balloons; water; sink with a faucet

What to Do:
1. Fill up all the water balloons and tie them off.
2. Carefully place the balloons in the aquarium until it is full.
3. Pour in enough water to cover the balloons.

Explanation: Your model resembles a tiny group of animal cells. Real animal cells are surrounded by fluid. Animal cells are round in shape. Cells are tiny compartments that make up all living things. Animals have numerous different types of cells, and each one has a special job. Actual cells are so small you cannot see them with your eyes.

Breathing Easy

Purpose: To model how the diaphragm of the lung works in an animal.

Time: 10 minutes

What You'll Need: small, plastic beverage bottle, wrapper removed; small amount of molding clay; 2 flexible straws; 3 balloons (2 small and one 9-inch circular); scissors; duct tape

Safety: Use caution when working with scissors.

What to Do:

1. Cut the bottom off of the bottle.
2. Remove the small plastic ring left from the twist top.
3. Use duct tape to cover the cut bottom edge of the bottle (around the rim only).
4. Tape the straws together and bend the flexible necks slightly away from each other.
5. Insert the ends of the straws nearest the flexible necks into small balloons.
6. Tape each balloon to its straw for an airtight fit.
7. Insert straws through the open bottom and through the neck of the bottle, balloon ends down.
8. Fasten the straws to the neck of the bottle with the clay. Make it airtight.
9. Cut the 9-inch balloon at the neck. Stretch the balloon over the open bottom of the bottle and secure it with duct tape.
10. Push and pull on the bottom to illustrate the diaphragm in contracted and relaxed positions.

Explanation: Pushing the balloon covering in (diaphragm is relaxed) creates high air pressure and empties the balloon lungs. Pulling the balloon covering (diaphragm is contracted) creates low air pressure within the cavity and air rushes in to fill the lungs. All animals on this planet, including man, use this procedure to breathe.

Fly Away Little Birdie

Purpose: To show how a bird flies.

Time: 2 minutes

What You'll Need: book; strip of paper, 10 inches long by 2 inches wide

What to Do:
1. Place about one inch of the paper strip in the middle of the closed book. The rest of the paper should hang over the edge.
2. Hold the book up so that the paper is below your mouth.
3. Blow gently across the top of the paper for a few seconds.
4. Now blow harder.

Explanation: The paper moves up. As a current of air flows across the top of a bird's outstretched wing, there is a change in pressure. The difference in pressure above and below the bird's wing produces an upward force that causes the wing to rise. When you blew on top of the paper, you decreased the pressure while the pressure below the paper was higher.

I Can't Make Any Sense Out of This

Purpose: To display how the sense of smell is used to taste foods.

Time: 1 minute

What You'll Need: peppermint-flavored gum, your nose and fingers

What to Do:
1. Unwrap the gum.
2. Hold your nose with two fingers and put the gum into your mouth.
3. Chew the gum while holding your nose and try to identify the flavor.
4. Remove your fingers from your nose and now try to identify the flavor.
5. (Optional) Try this with other types of food.

Explanation: Much of what the human animal can smell is actually odor. This is true of certain flavors. Peppermint has an odor, but not a taste. Most animals have excellent senses of smell, much better than humans.

Noisy Bugs

Purpose: To illustrate how some types of insects make noise.

Time: 1 minute

What You'll Need: fingernail file or emery board, index card

What to Do:
1. Hold the index card upright with one lone edge resting on a table.
2. Support the card with one hand as you draw the rough side of the file across the card quickly several times.

Explanation: Explain that the vibrations between the file and the card cause the rasping sound you hear. Certain insects, like crickets and grasshoppers, produce sounds in much the same way. These insects make sounds by rubbing two body parts against each other.

Over the Lips and Through the Gums

Purpose: To demonstrate the difference in physical and chemical changes within the digestive tract.

Time: 1 minute

What You'll Need: tasty food snack (keep in mind potential allergies any students might have and plan accordingly)

What to Do:
1. Take the treat and break it in half.
2. Place the treat in your mouth and chew it for 30 seconds.
3. Swallow the treat.
4. Discuss the physical and chemical changes that have occurred.

Explanation: When you broke the treat in half, you did not produce anything new. It was the same treat. This is called a physical change. However, when you chew the treat, it started to chemically react with the saliva in your mouth. Eating the treat did produce a new product and was therefore a chemical change. All animals use the process of digesting food for energy and for cell development and it starts at the beginning of the digestive tract, which is the mouth.

HANDS-ON BOTANY

Botany is a branch of biology that includes the scientific study of plant life and development. The science of botany covers a wide range of disciplines that study plants, algae, and fungi, and includes structure, growth, reproduction, metabolism, development, diseases, and the chemical properties and evolutionary relationships between these different groups. This study begins with basic efforts to identify edible, medicinal, and poisonous plants, making botany one of the oldest of the sciences. Botany includes the study of more than a half-million different kinds or species of living organisms.

Nothing says Mother Nature more than a field trip to a local forest preserve, arboretum, or botanic gardens. When you observe the quality and quantity of vegetation, you may wonder how this environment is related to the world around us. In the unit, students will be able to act like botanists—scientists who interpret and study plants—and draw specific conclusions about the many factors that make up a plant.

Lessons

Celery Stalker

Purpose: To illustrate through osmosis how plants absorb water and food.

Time: 5 minutes, plus waiting time

What You'll Need: stalk of celery with its leaves, glass of water, red food coloring, bright light, tablespoon

What to Do:
1. Mix about one tablespoon of red food coloring into the glass of water.
2. Place the stalk of celery into the glass.
3. Place it in a bright light and let it remain overnight.
4. Observe what happens.
5. (Optional) Repeat the activity with other vegetables.

Explanation: The leaves turn a reddish color. The celery stalk is the stem of the celery. It absorbs water and minerals from the soil through its root hairs by a process called osmosis. Osmosis occurs when some liquids and gases pass through a skin-like membrane. Water passes into all of the cells and is carried up through its center tubes to the plant's stems and leaves.

Chlorophyll Capers

Purpose: To demonstrate that plants contain chlorophyll.

Time: 15 minutes, plus waiting time

What You'll Need: 7–10 spinach leaves, 2 cups of water, stove, sauce pan or pot, slotted spoon, clear glass

Safety: Use caution when working with boiling water on a stove.

What to Do:
1. Heat the water until it comes to a boil.
2. With the spoon, place the spinach leaves in the pot and pour in the water.
3. Continue heating until you notice the water turning green.
4. Remove the pot from the stove and allow cooling.
5. Remove the spinach from the pot.
6. Pour the water into the glass.
7. Observe the results.
8. (Optional) Repeat this experiment with other green plants and observe what happens.

Explanation: The green-colored material is a chemical called chlorophyll. Chlorophyll is a substance found in plants that captures light that is necessary for triggering chemical reactions in the process of photosynthesis.

Don't Cry for These Cells

Purpose: To observe an onion cell.

Time: 5 minutes

What You'll Need: small, fresh onion; magnifying glass; knife; tweezers; clean windowpane of glass

Safety: Use extreme caution when cutting the onion.

What to Do:
1. Cut a small square out of the onion.
2. Use the tweezers; gently pull away a thin film of onion skin.
3. Press the onion skin onto a windowpane so it sticks in position.
4. Observe the skin through your magnifying glass.

Explanation: You should be able to see rectangular shaped cells. Plant cells are not the same as animal cells. Animal cells are soft and flexible, whereas plant cells have a tough outer wall that give them a fixed round shape. Plant cells are usually much larger than animal cells, which makes them easier to see.

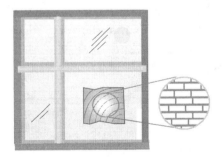

Down They Go

Purpose: To observe root pattern formations.

Time: 10 minutes, plus waiting time

What You'll Need: flat, Styrofoam food container; wet paper towels; 6 fresh popcorn kernels; plastic wrap

What to Do:
1. Lay several wet paper towels on the food container.
2. Spread the popcorn kernels on the wet paper towels with their root (the pointed end) each facing the same direction.
3. Tightly seal the entire container with the plastic wrap so no water can leak out.
4. Stand the bed on its edge so the pointed ends of the kernels are pointing down.
5. Allow them to grow for several days and notice how the roots are growing.
6. Turn the bed 90 degrees every 2–3 days and observe the results. Do this several times.
7. (Optional) Repeat this activity with other dried seeds.

Explanation: No matter what direction you turn the seeds, they always turn downward. After a week or so, the roots will make an interesting pattern. When a seedling grows in soil, its roots go downward. If something is in the way, the roots will move around it and keep on going down—even if you point the roots up, they turn back.

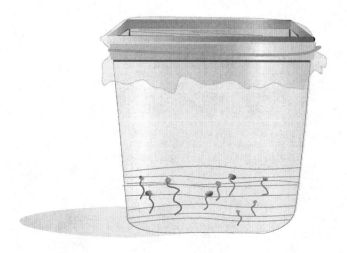

Fuzzy Math for Trees

Purpose: To calculate the age of a tree.

Time: 5 minutes

What You'll Need: several different nonevergreen trees, tape measure, calculator (optional)

What to Do:
1. Hold the tape measure about 3 feet above the ground and measure the distance around the tree. This provides an approximate age of the tree.

Explanation: By measuring around the trunk of a tree, you can get an estimate of its age. Trees grow at different rates. The circumference (distance around the tree) of a mature tree increases about one inch every year. Palm trees and some fast-growing trees, such as conifers, do not follow this guide.

Gimme' Some Air

Purpose: To show the process of photosynthesis.

Time: 2 minutes, plus waiting time

What You'll Need: clear bowl, clear jar that fits inside the bowl, several weeds or plants from a pond or lake, water, sunny spot

What to Do:
1. Fill the bowl about halfway with water.
2. Place the plants in the bowl of water.
3. Place the jar upside down in the bowl.
4. Push the plants into the jar, and then rest the jar on the bottom of the bowl. The plants should be covered by water in the inverted jar.
5. Leave the bowl in bright sunlight for several hours.
6. Observe what happens.
7. (Optional) Try this with other plants such as flowers or grass clippings.

Explanation: Bubbles of oxygen start to rise to the water surface. Plants give off oxygen in a complex process called photosynthesis. This takes place in the green portion of the plant. To survive, all animals use this release of oxygen from a plant.

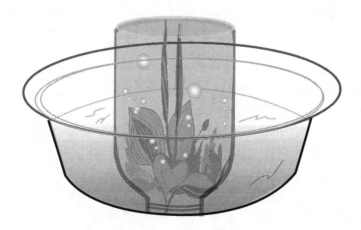

I'm Cracking Up

Purpose: To determine the strength of a plant root system.

Time: 10 minutes, plus waiting time

What You'll Need: potting soil; several raw eggs and the egg carton; marigold flower seeds; small spoon; water; warm, light environment

What to Do:
1. Carefully crack an egg from the top, dispose of the insides, and peel back the eggshell so you have a half eggshell.
2. Gently using the spoon, fill the half eggshell to the top with the soil. Do this with several eggshells if you wish.
3. Place the eggshell(s) back into the egg carton.
4. Sprinkle seeds on the top and cover them with a little soil.
5. Place them in a warm, light location and water every day. Do not overwater.
6. After the seeds start to germinate, lift your eggshell flowerpot and look at the bottom.
7. (Optional) Repeat with other plant seeds.

Explanation: The root system has forced and broken its way through the bottom of the eggshell. Some roots are so strong that they can even push through cracks in rock formations.

Now Ear This!

Purpose: To observe corn growth directly on the ear.

Time: 2 minutes, plus waiting time

What You'll Need: fresh ear of corn, pan, water

What to Do:
1. Fill the pan about half full of water.
2. Remove any husk on the corn. Place the ear of corn in the water.
3. Replace the water every few days with fresh water. Flush the old water down the drain.
4. Observe what happens.
5. (Optional) Continue the growth process for several more weeks or months.

Explanation: Kernels of corn will begin to split and sprout in the pan. A corncob is made of many seeds. When placed in water, the seeds will soak up the water and they will sprout and grow in much the same way a farmer plants corn in the ground.

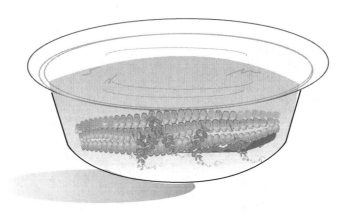

Orange You Glad

Purpose: To taste different parts of an orange to determine sugar content.

Time: 2 minutes

What You'll Need: orange, knife, your mouth

What to Do:
1. Peel the orange.
2. Cut one slice across the stem and then one slice across the blossom end.
3. Taste the slices and compare the sugar content of each.
4. (Optional) Repeat Steps 1–3 with other fruits and compare the sugar content of the orange with the other fruits you sample.

Explanation: The blossom end of the orange is sweeter because it develops more sugar due to its increased exposure to the sun. For this reason, fruits grown in the temperate zone are only 10–15% sugars whereas those from the tropics, such as bananas, figs, and dates, are about 20–60% sugar.

Pine Cone Pixies

Purpose: To determine if pine cones contain seeds.

Time: 5 minutes

What You'll Need: several young evergreen pine cones (cones with tightly closed scales), clean towel or rag, sheet of newsprint

Note: If the pinecones are located in trees on private property, obtain permission from the owner before taking them.

What to Do:
1. Spread out the newspaper.
2. Wrap the towel around the end of one of the pinecones.
3. Hold the toweled end in each hand and twist the cone back and forth several times to loosen its scales. (If this is too difficult, soak the cones in water for a few hours.)
4. While holding the base of the cone with the towel with one hand, use your fingers from the other hand to pull out several scales near the tip of the cone.

Explanation: Two seeds, each attached to a paper-like wing, are found on the inside of the scales of the pinecone. Pinecones contain seeds of a pine tree. Pine trees are conifers, which are nonflowering plants that reproduce by forming cones. Most conifers are evergreens. That is, their leaves stay green on the trees all year.

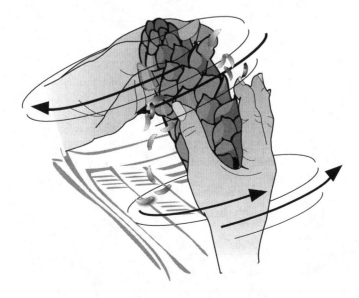

Popcorn Push-Ups

Purpose: To observe how popcorn seeds absorb water.

Time: 5+ minutes

What You'll Need: bag of fresh, unpopped popcorn kernels; clear jar; plastic dish; water

What to Do:
1. Fill the jar with water and then pour in the unpopped popcorn kernels so they reach the top.
2. Cover the jar with the dish.
3. Check back in an hour and then again the next day.
4. Observe the results.
5. (Optional) Repeat Steps 1–3 with other types of dried seeds. Always start with a fresh water container for each type of seed.

Explanation: The kernels will have pushed off the dish by the next day. Outdoors, seeds are weigh-lifters, too. When a seed swells with water, pressure builds on it. The seeds push aside soil, making room for the baby plant's root and stem.

Sour Apple Juice

Purpose: To test how apple juice changes into vinegar.

Time: 10+ minutes

What You'll Need: 8-ounce glass of apple juice; small, clear jar; baking soda; tablespoon

What to Do:
1. Pour the apple juice into a glass and allow it to sit undisturbed for a few days.
2. Each day, test the apple juice by removing 2–3 tablespoons of the juice and placing it into the small jar.
3. Add a pinch of baking soda to the jar. If bubbles form, vinegar is present.
4. (Optional) Try this experiment with other types of fruit juices.

Explanation: The bubbling of the baking soda with the old apple juice means you no longer have apple juice. It has turned into acetic acid or vinegar. Some companies use apple juice to make vinegar. Small growing microbes can make the sugar in apple juice turn into vinegar. This is a chemical reaction that produces carbon dioxide gas, which is the foam you observed.

Tree Power

Purpose: To demonstrate the strength of paper.

Time: 5 minutes

What You'll Need: corrugated cardboard box, scissors, large fruit juice can, masking tape, small board (cutting board) to stand on, partner

Safety: Use caution when cutting the cardboard.

What to Do:
1. Cut a strip from the box about 4 inches in height and about 12 inches long.
2. Wrap the strip around the juice can and tape it.
3. Slide the can off of the strip.
4. Place the board on top of the cardboard circle. Center it.
5. With your partner at your side, carefully stand in the center of the board.

Explanation: The cardboard circle supports your total weight. The strength of the paper, which comes from a living tree, comes from the combination of circular shape and the corrugated paper.

Water Lilies

Purpose: To display how water moves through plant vascular tissue.

Time: 5 minutes

What You'll Need: sheet of plain paper, scissors, crayons or colored pencils, bowl of water

Attention: Use caution when working with scissors.

What to Do:
1. Draw a large-sized lily with at least 10 long petals protruding from the center of the flower.
2. Color your flower.
3. Cut out the flower along the solid lines.
4. Fold the petals firmly into the center.
5. Place the lily on the water and observe.
6. (Optional) Take the leaves of a wilted plant and repeat Step 5.

Explanation: The petals of the lily slowly open. These paper petals protruding from the center of the flower consist mostly of plant fibers that are made up of very small capillary tubes. As the water rises in these tubes, the paper begins to swell and the petals open.

You Have a Lot of Gall

Purpose: To observe what is inside a gall.

Time: 5 minutes

What You'll Need: tree galls (look like swellings on the leaves and/or stems of a birch, blueberry, elm, oak, pecan, or willow tree), magnifying glass, knife, cutting board

Safety: Use caution when cutting through the gall.

Note: If the plant is on someone's private property, obtain permission before taking the galls.

What to Do:
1. Remove several leaves or stems with galls from the trees.
2. Carefully cut each gall in half.
3. Look at them using your magnifying glass.

Explanation: The gall may be empty or may contain insects in various stages of development such as eggs, larvae, pupae, or adults. A gall is an abnormal swelling or thickening on a plant. Galls can occur anywhere on a plant and may be nearly solid or almost hollow.

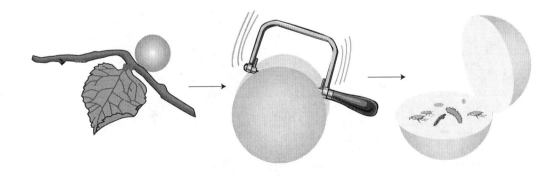

You're All Wet

Purpose: To demonstrate how overwatering plants can be a problem.

Time: 5 minutes, plus waiting time

What You'll Need: rhubarb stalks (found in the produce section of the grocery store), bowl of water, undisturbed place

What to Do:
1. Place several stalks of rhubarb in the bowl of water.
2. Leave the rhubarb undisturbed for one day.
3. Observe what happens.
4. (Optional) Try this with other vegetables.

Explanation: The ends of the stalks are split and curly. Rhubarb stalks contain cells that absorb water at different rates. Some of these cells absorb more water than others, causing them to swell open and split apart. Many plants have these special types of cells, which is why you never want to overwater a plant, because too much water, like too little water, can kill the plant.

HANDS-ON ENTOMOLOGY

Entomology is the scientific study of insects. Scientist have identified more than 1.3 million species of insects, which account for more than two thirds of all known organisms that date back some 400 million years. Insects have frequent everyday encounters and interactions with us humans and other forms of life on Earth. Entomology is considered a specialty scientific area within the field of biology.

This section will put a whole new meaning to the phrase, "What's buggin' you?" As insects are the most abundant species on our planet, you are never more than a few feet away from one. Yuck! For folks who are bothered by these interesting little creatures, that might be a bit worrisome. But do not fear. After completing just a few of these activities, students will have a much better understanding of these wonderful creepy crawlers.

Lessons

Ants in Your Pants

Purpose: To observe an ant colony.

Time: 20 minutes, plus observation time

What You'll Need: 2 cups of very fine soil, quart-size wide-mouth jar, long-handled mixing spoon, cotton ball moistened with tap water, apple wedge, 6 × 6-inch square cloth, rubber band, tape, scissors, black construction paper, 25–30 ants (from an outdoor anthill), cool area

Safety: Use special care when working with ants. Do not allow them to get on your skin. Do not do this experiment if you are allergic to ants.

What to Do:
1. Pour the soil into the jar.
2. Locate an anthill and use the long-handled mixing spoon to stir up the top of an anthill.
3. When the ants run out, scoop up a few dozen of them and place them into the jar.
4. Quickly moisten the cotton ball and drop it into the jar along with the apple wedge.
5. Immediately cover the jar with the cloth.
6. Use the rubber band to secure the cloth to the jar.
7. Cut the construction paper to make a tube that fits loosely around the outside of the jar. The tube should be about 2 inches higher than the soil inside the jar.
8. Place your ant colony in a cool area.
9. Several times a day for about a week, slide the tube off the jar and observe.

Explanation: You will notice that at first the ants will frantically run around the jar before they settle down. Some will begin digging almost immediately. By the end of the week, clearly defined tunnels are visible in the soil and small anthills dot the surface. Ants are insects that live in colonies.

At a Snail's Pace

Purpose: To study the movement of snails.

Time: 10 minutes, plus observation time

What You'll Need: several snails (from a pet shop or garden), large clay flowerpot or other similar object, enamel paint, thin paintbrush

What to Do:
1. Pick up a snail and tap it gently to make it pull in its body.
2. Paint a number on the back, starting with 1, on each snail. Be careful not to get any paint on the snail's body.
3. Lay the flowerpot on its side.
4. Place all of the snails in the flowerpot and observe their movement for a short time.
5. Come back a few hours later and see where they are.

Explanation: What you actually accomplished in this activity is some wildlife tracking. You should have noticed that the snails like to rest in damp places. By marking animals, scientists can show how far they travel.

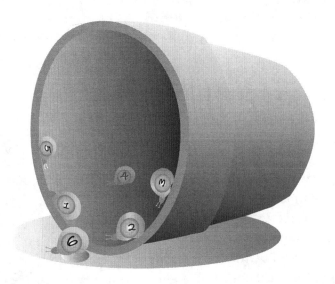

Candy Bugs You Can Eat

Purpose: To make a model of an adult insect's three main body parts.

Time: 10 minutes

What You'll Need: 6 gumdrops, 9 round toothpicks

What to Do:
1. Place three gumdrops on one toothpick. This is your insect's abdomen.
2. Place two gumdrops on another toothpick. This is your insect's thorax.
3. Push the gumdrops firmly against each other and break off any part of the toothpick that is sticking out any end.
4. Attach a single gumdrop—the head—to the thorax with a toothpick. Then attach the thorax to the abdomen with another toothpick.
5. At an angle, place two toothpicks opposite each other in the thorax and place four toothpicks, set opposite each other, in the abdomen.
6. Position your insect so it is standing on all 6 legs.
7. Break a toothpick in half and use the pieces as the antenna on the head.

Clean Up: Remove the toothpicks and eat them—Yum!

Explanation: An adult insect is divided into three main body parts, the head, thorax, and abdomen. The head is the front part, the thorax is in the middle, and the abdomen takes up the rear. The abdomen is divided into even smaller segments, just like your gumdrop model. All insects have six legs. If it does not have six legs, like a spider, which has eight legs, it is not an insect.

Flying Fruit Flies

Purpose: To create a fruit fly habitat.

Time: 10 minutes, plus observation time

What You'll Need: glass jar; 6 × 6 inch piece of cloth; rubber band; very ripe banana; warm, bright place

What to Do:
1. Cut a very ripe banana into several pieces, keeping them on the peel.
2. Place the banana pieces in the jar and place the jar in a very warm and bright place until the banana turns black. Do not cover the jar.
3. After the banana turns black, fasten the cloth over the jar with the rubber band and check it every few days.
4. If the banana has been visited by fruit flies, the eggs will soon hatch. If it is warm, they will turn into flies in about 10 days.

Explanation: Insects live on an amazing variety of foods. In the summer, fruit flies wander through the air searching for a suitable place to lay their eggs. The decaying banana has changed the chemical composition of the fruit, so it will attract female fruit flies that are ready to lay eggs.

Heads or Tails?

Purpose: To determine the head and tail of an earthworm.

Time: 2 minutes

What You'll Need: plate, pencil, water, long earthworm

What to Do:
1. Rinse the plate to make it wet.
2. Gently place the earthworm on it.
3. With the pencil, lightly touch one end of the worm.
4. Immediately touch the other end.
5. Observe which end moves the fastest.

Explanation: The side that moves the quickest is the tail. A worm's tail is extremely sensitive to touch. If a bird touches a worm's tail, the worm will suddenly contract and pull its whole body underground in order to escape. When you touch the head, the worm reaction is much slower. A worm has two sets of muscles that enable it to move.

How Flies Eat—Yuck!

Purpose: To model how flies eat their food.

Time: 5 minutes, plus wait time

What You'll Need: jar of sweet potato baby food, eyedropper, masking tape, pen, your saliva, refrigerator

What to Do:
1. Place the tip of the eyedropper just below the surface of the baby food in the jar.
2. Try to fill the eyedropper with the sweet potato.
3. Wash the dropper.
4. Collect as much saliva in your mouth as possible and carefully drool the saliva onto the surface of the sweet potato jar.
5. Close the jar. Place a piece of tape across the lid and down the side. Label the tape: DO NOT EAT.
6. Place the jar in the refrigerator and leave it undisturbed for 24 hours.
7. Remove the jar and repeat Step 1 and observe what happens.
8. Try this with other soft food.

Explanation: At first, you were unable to draw any of the sweet potato into the eyedropper. However, after the saliva was in the jar for 24 hours, the potato became liquid and easily drew into the dropper. Human saliva, like the saliva of flies—and many other insects—contains a chemical called amylase. This breaks down starch, a complex chemical found in many foods, into simpler materials.

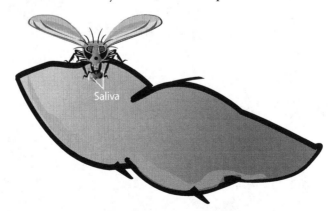

Saliva

Spider Art

Purpose: To capture a spider web.

Time: 5 minutes

What You'll Need: aerosol can of hair spray, spider web (make sure the spider is not in the web), sheet of cardboard

What to Do:
1. Find a spider web. Spider webs can be found in and around the school and neighborhood. Check around cool, damp locations in undisturbed areas.
2. Gently spray the entire web with the aerosol spray.
3. Spray the cardboard with the spray.
4. Quickly press the wet cardboard against the web and pull it away.
5. Allow the web to dry.

Explanation: When you sprayed on the hair spray, the hair spray particles stuck directly onto the web surface, which in turn caused the web to stick to the cardboard. It was easier to see the pattern of the web once it was on the surface of the paper. Carefully observe the patterns. Do you see any that are identical?

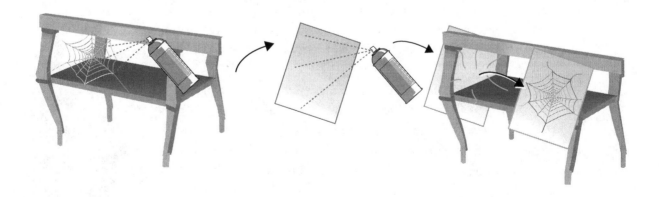

Wacky Science © Prufrock Press

Permission is granted to photocopy or reproduce this page for classroom use only.

41

The Worms Move in, the Worms Move out

Purpose: To observe the preferred environment of earthworms.

Time: 20 minutes, plus wait time

What You'll Need: 2 cups of dark-colored soil, one cup of light-colored sand, tablespoon of oats, dark-colored construction paper, large bowl, water, spoon, quart-size wide-mouth jar, rubber band, about 5–8 earthworms (from the bait store, your lawn after a thunderstorm, or a garden or wooded area), cool location

What to Do:

1. Pour the soil in the bowl.
2. Slowly add water until the soil is slightly moist.
3. Pour half of the soil into the jar.
4. Pour the sand over the soil.
5. Add the remaining soil.
6. Sprinkle the oats over the soil.
7. Put the worms in the jar.
8. Wrap the paper around the jar and secure it with the rubber band. Place in a cool location.
9. Every day for a week, remove the paper and observe the jar. Put the paper back and return the jar to the cool location.

Explanation: The worms start wiggling and burrow into the soil. After a few days, tunnels can be seen in the soil, and the dark soil and light sand become mixed. Worms live in and eat their way through soil. They get nourishment from the remains of other living things. Worms move about and loosen the soil so that water and air needed by plants can easily pass through.

You're Buggin' Me

Purpose: To see how food is used to make an animal shelter.

Time: 10 minutes, plus wait time

What You'll Need: grapefruit; knife; warm, undisturbed area around your classroom or school

What to Do:
1. Slice the grapefruit in half and remove the fleshy fruit so you are left with only the skin.
2. Place the grapefruit skin outside, hollow side down, in an undisturbed area on some bare ground.
3. Allow to sit overnight.
4. Turn over the grapefruit skin and observe.

Explanation: The skin is tough and full of juices. The juice will make the air underneath the fruit moist and attract a lot of small animals. Slugs come out at night searching for food.

HANDS-ON HUMAN ANIMAL SCIENCE

On Earth, there exist about 5,000 species of living mammals. These mammals are divided into three subclasses with about 26 different orders. Mammals have body hair, have three middle ear bones (hammer, anvil, and stirrup) and nourish their young with milk that females produce in modified sweat glands that are called mammary glands.

When thinking about animals, many people do not think of themselves. But the human being is a mammal. That collection also includes apes and other four-legged animals, whales, dolphins, and bats. This section takes a look at certain behaviors of humans and how we interact with the world around us.

Lessons

Disappearing Act

Purpose: To demonstrate that every animal has a blind spot in each eye.

Time: 5 minutes

What You'll Need: the box at the bottom of the page, your eyes

What to Do:

1. Hold the X/O rectangle at the bottom of this page in your right hand at arm's length.
2. Make sure that the X is directly in front of your right eye. Close your left eye.
3. Slowly move the X/O rectangle toward your right eye while continuing to stare at the center of the X.
4. At some point the O will disappear; stop moving the paper when this occurs. This is your blind spot. (If the O never disappears, then the rectangle was moved too fast or your eyes were moving around. Try it several times.)
5. To find the left eye's blind spot, hold the O in front of the left eye and close the right eye and repeat Step 3, except stare at the O this time.

Explanation: Every animal has a blind spot on the back of the interior of its eye. It is found where the retina meets the optic nerve. At this point, there are no rods and cones or nerve endings to gather light to send to the brain.

X ☐ O

I'm Falling for You

Purpose: To determine how other body parts affect balance.

Time: 3 minutes

What You'll Need: large, soft pillow or cushion; blindfold; partner

Safety: Have your partner near to spot you so you do not fall.

What to Do:
1. Stand on the pillow with your arms held out.
2. Now stand on one leg, keeping your arms outstretched.
3. Put on the blindfold and stand on one leg, keeping your arms outstretched.
4. Now hold your arms by your side.
5. Remove the blindfold and repeat Steps 4 and 5.

Explanation: The pillow separates your feet from the ground, making it slightly more difficult for you to stand upright. When you stand on one leg, your brain has only half of the information necessary to keep you balanced. With the blindfold, without clues from your eyes to report the position of your head in relation to its surroundings, your brain has a more difficult time telling if you are upright. With your arms at their sides, you completely lose your balance.

I Vant to Suck Your Blood

Purpose: To observe how gravity affects blood flow.

Time: 3 minutes

What You'll Need: yourself

Safety: Do not attempt this activity if you have a balance problem or if you are prone to fainting.

What to Do:
1. Hold one hand up in the air as high as you can, and let the other hand hang down. Do this for at least 2 minutes.
2. Hold both hands next to each other, palms up, and compare the two.

Explanation: You should find that the higher hand is paler in color than the lower hand. The difference in color is caused by gravity. It drains blood out of the higher hands, but holds it back in the lower hand. Your heart needs to work harder to pump blood to your hand above your head.

No Need to Be So Loud

Purpose: Determines how sound is amplified inside the ear.

Time: 5 minutes

What You'll Need: metal spoon, 2 feet of string, table

What to Do:
1. Tie the handle of the spoon in the center of the string.
2. Wrap the ends of the string around both index fingers. Make sure that both strings are the same length.
3. Place the tip of each index finger in each ear.
4. Lean over so that the spoon hangs freely and tap it against the side of the table.
5. Observe what happens.
6. (Optional) Change the length and tap it against other objects.

Explanation: The sound from the spoon amplifies into your ears and sounds like a church bell. The metal in the spoon starts to vibrate, and these vibrations are transmitted up the string to your ears. The ability for animals to hear is due to their ability to transmit vibrations. Most animals hear more clearly than humans, so their ability to pick up vibrations is much more sensitive.

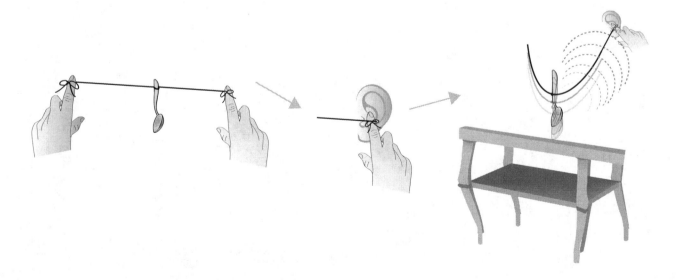

Peeeeee-u

Purpose: To exhibit the sense of smell.

Time: 2 minutes

What You'll Need: balloon, vanilla extract

What to Do:
1. Blow up the balloon and then quickly pour a small amount of vanilla extract into the balloon and tie if off.
2. Shake the balloon for about 30 seconds.
3. Smell the balloon.
4. (Optional) Blow up other balloons and try other scents.

Explanation: The outside of the balloon smells like vanilla. The vanilla molecules actually pass through the walls of the balloon even though it was sealed off. There is enough space between the molecules of the balloon to let the vanilla molecules, which are very small, pass through. An animal's sense of smell is much more accurate than a human being's sense of smell.

Wash Those Hands!

Purpose: To validate the importance of hand washing.

Time: 5 minutes

What You'll Need: blue tempera paint, soap, sink, bar or liquid soap, blindfold, water, container, spoon, timer, a partner

What to Do:

1. Mix up a diluted solution of tempera paint, with half paint and half water.
2. Dip your hand into the container of paint and allow it to dry. Be careful not to drip the paint on anyone or anything.
3. Have your partner blindfold you.
4. Stand over the sink, have your partner place the soap in your hand, turn on the water, and wash your hands for exactly one minute.
5. Remove the blindfold and look at your hands.
6. Repeat Step 4, but without the blindfold, and look at your hands again.

Explanation: The remaining blue paint on your hands represents bacteria. Even after washing your hands several times, some of the paint remains. You think your hands are clean, but they really are not. It is important for everyone to thoroughly wash their hands before each meal and to never place your hands in your mouth.

You Are What You Eat

Purpose: To understand the meaning of a food label.

Time: 10 minutes

What You'll Need: several boxes or packages of your favorite foods

What to Do:
1. Turn to the side or back of the food package that is labeled "Nutrition Facts."
2. Carefully read the label from top to bottom. Pay close attention to the items that are in bold, including "% Daily Value."
3. (Optional) For an entire day, calculate the total amount of fat, saturated fat, cholesterol, and sodium you consume. Then check the labels at the bottom of the Nutrition Facts to see if your diet (assume 2,500 calories) is within that range.

Explanation: All plants and animals use food for energy. For humans, a healthy diet should consist of no more than 30% calories from fat. The lower the total fat, saturated fat, cholesterol, and sodium numbers are on the label, the better the food is for you.

Nutrition Facts

Serving Size 1/2 cup (200g)
Servings Per Container About 10

Amount Per Serving

Calories 250   **Calories from Fat** 80

	% Daily Value
Total Fat 10g	**15%**
Saturated Fat 1g	**5%**
Cholesterol 0g	**0%**
Sodium 220g	**9%**
Total Carbohydrate 80g	**27%**
Dietary Fiber 3g	**12%**
Sugars 70g	
Protein 2g	

Vitamin A 0%	•	Vitamin C 10%	
Calcium 2%	•	Iron 10%	

Percent Daily Values are based on a 2,000 calorie diet. Your daily values may be higher or lower depending on your calorie needs:

	Calories	2,000	2,500
Total Fat	Less than	65g	80g
Sat Fat	Less than	20g	80g
Cholesterol	Less than	300mg	300mg
Sodium	Less than	2,400mg	2,400mg
Total Carbohydrate		300g	375g
Dietary Fiber		25g	30g

HANDS-ON PALEONTOLOGY

Paleontology is the study of what fossils tell us about the ecologies of the past, about evolution, and about our place, as humans, in the world. Paleontology incorporates knowledge from past and current studies of biology, geology, ecology, anthropology, archaeology, and even computer science. This helps us to understand the processes that have led to the origination and eventual destruction of the different types of organisms since life arose.

The science of paleontology attempts to answer questions such as, "Where did we come from?" and "What makes us human?" Paleontology includes the study of ancient life using fossil confirmation. Scientists have developed our theory of evolution by studying the ancient life of thousands of types of plant and animal fossils, including dinosaur fossils. In this section, students will have the opportunity to actually perform similar activities that scientists have used to develop different theories of prehistoric times.

Lessons

A Sticky Situation

Purpose: To model how tree ember seals fossils.

Time: 2 minutes, plus wait time

What You'll Need: jar of honey or clear corn syrup, several dead insects or small plant leaves, freezer, spoon

What to Do:
1. Place the insects and/or plant leaves inside the jar of honey or corn syrup.
2. Make sure they are evenly spaced throughout the jar.
3. Place jar in the freezer with the top on for several hours.
4. Observe what happens.

Explanation: The specimens are very solid and encased inside the thick jar of honey or syrup. Resin is a gooey secretion of plants, particularly coniferous trees. It is valued for its chemical materials and uses, such as varnishes and adhesives, and as an important source of raw materials for items such as nail polish, incense, and perfume. Fossilized resins, represented by your honey or syrup, are the source of amber. These sticky resin materials trapped fossils millions of years ago.

Animal Trackers in My Soup

Purpose: To preserve an animal track.

Time: 10 minutes, plus wait time

What You'll Need: plastic bag, one-pound bag of plaster of Paris, water, container, large spoon or small shovel

Safety: Mix the plaster of Paris carefully and avoid getting it in your eyes.

What to Do:
1. Visit a muddy pond and look for a complete animal footprint.
2. Pour the plaster of Paris in the container and add the water slowly until the mixture looks like cream gravy.
3. Carefully pour the plaster over the entire track.
4. Allow the plaster to harden for about 30 minutes. Attempt to figure out which type of animal track you have.
5. When the top is dry, dig up the plaster track and rinse it with some water.
6. (Optional) Make a plaster cast of your own footprint or handprint.

Explanation: Many fossils are no more than animal footprints that have been preserved for thousands of years. Fossil scientists who study the size and habits of many animals use this procedure for cast making.

Fingerprint IDs

Purpose: To observe tracks of wild animals.

Time: 5 minutes, plus wait time

What You'll Need: fine grain sand; ruler; thin baking tray or pan; forest preserve, wooded area, garden, or other open outdoor area

What to Do:
1. Pour the sand in the tray and use the ruler to smooth it out.
2. Find an undisturbed outdoor nature area and place the tray down. Keep it there overnight.
3. Check for animal track marks and try to identify them.
4. (Optional) Smooth out the sand and observe for several more days.

Explanation: Small round paw prints without claw marks are from cats. Raccoons, badgers, or other night animals make bigger prints with claw marks. If the tracks are evenly spaced, the animal was walking or running. If there are a pair of prints together, the animal was hopping. The deeper the tracks, the larger the animal.

Wacky Science © Prufrock Press

Permission is granted to photocopy or reproduce this page for classroom use only.

55

Crazy Clay Fossil

Purpose: To use heat to make a fossil.

Time: 15 minutes, plus wait time

What You'll Need: modeling clay, small plastic dinosaur, oven, knife

Safety: Use caution when working with a hot stove and a knife.

What to Do:
1. Preheat the oven to 150 degrees.
2. Roll the clay into a ball and cut it in half.
3. Press the plastic dinosaur into one half of the clay.
4. Cover the dinosaur with the other half of the clay and pinch the edges to close the clay together.
5. Bake the clay in the oven for about 30 minutes.
6. Remove the clay from the oven and allow time for cooling.
7. Crack open.
8. (Optional) Make a handprint or footprint fossil using the same procedure.

Explanation: Animal and plant remains become trapped in stone, leaving an imprint called a fossil. It takes millions of years for plants and animals to become fossilized.

Leave Me Alone

Purpose: To make impressions of tree leaves.

Time: 5 minutes

What You'll Need: variety of leaves, white sheets of paper, different colored crayons with the paper removed

What to Do:
1. Collect several different types of leaves.
2. Lay each leaf under a sheet of paper.
3. Gently rub over the leaf with the side of the crayon.
4. (Optional) Repeat this activity using the bark from the side of a tree.

Explanation: The indentations of the leaves leave an impression on the paper when you rub the crayon over them. These types of impressions can last many years, just like impressions made when soft rock sits over different types of plants and animals.

HANDS-ON PHYSICS

You may have heard the cliché that if it smells, it's chemistry; if it crawls, it's biology; and if it doesn't work, its physics. Well, we are going to take a glance into some basic physics principles—activities that actually work. Physics affects our everyday lives and it is interwoven into our daily events and behaviors—and most people really never think about it. Physics is the natural science that examines fundamental concepts such as energy and force, along with space-time and all that is derived from these concepts, such as mass, charge, matter, and its motion. Physics also is considered a general analysis and investigation of our natural world, which is conducted in an organized, prearranged manner that helps us understand how the world and universe behave. From the concepts of gravity to basic elemental structure, it is all physics, all the time. And remember, if it wasn't for Sir Isaac Newton, we would not have to eat bruised apples.

Lessons

Corn-Yuk

Purpose: To display the flexibility of cornstarch.

Time: 2 minutes

What You'll Need: 10 tablespoons of cornstarch, 5 tablespoons of water, plastic cup, spoon

What to Do:
1. Combine the cornstarch and water in the cup and stir. The mixture should appear to be solid. If not, add a pinch more cornstarch.
2. Jab your finger in the mixture very quickly.
3. Next, slowly place your finger in the mixture.
4. Compare how the two felt.
5. (Optional) Pour the mixture from one hand to the other, and then try to roll it into a ball.

Explanation: This material has properties of both a solid and a liquid, which we call a suspension. The amount of force you place on the material determines if it feels soft like a liquid or hard like a solid.

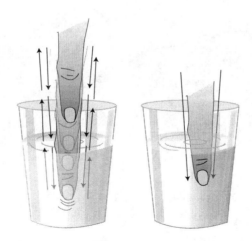

Dizzy Eggs

Purpose: To determine how to figure out when an egg is hard-boiled or raw.

Time: 1 minute

What You'll Need: raw egg, hard-boiled egg, smooth surface

What to Do:
1. Spin one of the eggs and watch it spin.
2. Spin the other egg with the same amount of force and watch it spin.
3. Compare what you saw.
4. (Optional) Partially cook an egg and spin it to see if it spins differently than a raw or hard-boiled egg.

Explanation: The hard-boiled egg spins in a nice smooth, even circle because it has a solid inside. The raw egg is a bit wobbly and will not spin as quickly because the egg is a fluid (not solid like the hard-boiled egg).

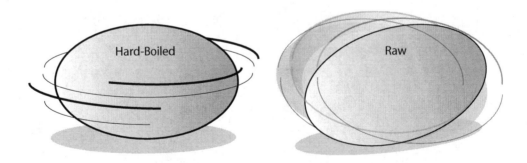

Goofy Grapes

Purpose: To show how gas particles adhere to the surface of raisins.

Time: 1 minute

What You'll Need: clear glass, clear carbonated beverage, dried raisins

What to Do:
1. Fill the glass ¾ full of beverage.
2. Drop in the raisins.

Explanation: Carbonated water contains dissolved carbon dioxide gas. The gas collects on the uneven surfaces of the raisins, which are dried grapes. When enough gas has collected, it will actually lift the raisins to the surface (like little parachutes) where the gas is then released into the air. With the gas gone, the raisins will sink back to the bottom, and the process starts all over again.

I'm Walkin' on Eggshells

Purpose: To demonstrate the strength of arches in supporting heavy loads using ordinary hen eggs.

Time: 10 minutes

What You'll Need: 4 raw eggs; clear tape; markers; small, sharp scissors; several books

Safety: Use caution when cutting the eggshells.

What to Do:
1. Carefully break off the smaller end of the eggs and remove the contents. Throw out the liquids inside, as well as the broken ends.
2. Rinse the shell domes and lightly dry.
3. Place the clear tape around the lower middle area of each shell.
4. Mark a line around the shell on the tape and cut along that line. Mark it as evenly as possible.
5. Place the four egg domes cut side down so that they form a rectangle.
6. Gently place a book on top of the four egg domes. Continue to add books until the eggshells crack.

Explanation: The domes of the eggshells distribute the mass of the books equally across the eggshells, both vertically and horizontally. The shape of an egg is like an arch. Arches have been used for about 2,000 years to support the great weights of bridges and cathedrals.

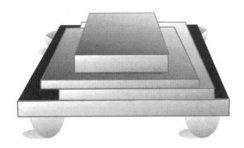

Orange Freeze

Purpose: To compare the freezing capacity of orange juice versus water.

Time: 2+ minutes

What You'll Need: orange juice, ice cube tray, freezer

What to Do:
1. Fill one half of the ice cube tray with orange juice and the other half with water.
2. Set in the freezer overnight.
3. Remove the frozen cubes.
4. Carefully bite into a cube of orange juice and a cube of water and compare.
5. (Optional) Try this with other fruit drinks.

Explanation: Both liquids lost heat energy when changing from a liquid to a solid. However, orange juice does not become as firm as the water. Many liquids, such as orange juice, have lower freezing points. There is a lot of water in the orange juice, and that froze; however, the actual juice was unfrozen, allowing you to easily eat the cube.

Paper Worm

Purpose: To display how some plants and animals absorb water.

Time: 1 minute

What You'll Need: straw with a paper wrapper, plate, water, eye dropper

What to Do:

1. Push the wrapper all the way down on one end of the straw.
2. Remove the crumpled wrapper and put it on the plate.
3. Place a few drops of water on the wrapper.

Explanation: The paper wrapper stretches and wiggles like a worm. The wrapper swells as it absorbs the drops of water. Simple animals and many plants absorb food and liquids through their skin, much like the paper.

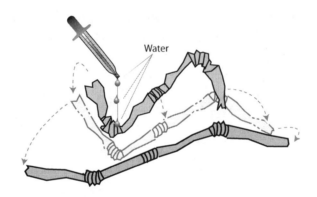

Water

Spider Tension

Purpose: To determine how a spider feels vibrations in its web.

Time: 5 minutes

What You'll Need: long piece of string, two stationary objects such as a table leg and a door, partner

What to Do:
1. Stretch the string tightly between the two stationary objects.
2. At one end of the string, gently place the tips of your fingers on the top of the string.
3. While you are looking the other way, have your partner pluck the opposite end of the string, starting lightly and then more firmly.

Explanation: You should be able to feel the varying degrees of vibration on your end of the string. A gentle touch produces a vibration, while the stronger the plucking, the more the string vibrates. Spiders feel the vibrations in their webs in much the same way. These webs act like telegraph lines and when the web shakes, the spider has senses on its legs to determine who or what is visiting him.

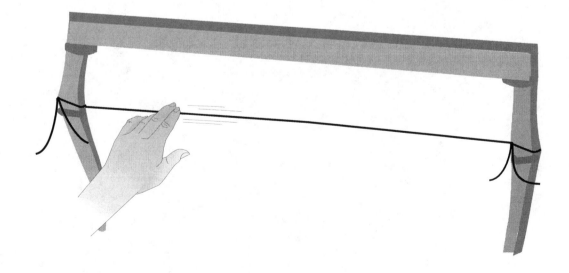

HANDS-ON ZOOLOGY

When you take a trip to the zoo, you are probably amused and excited when you watch the animals. You observe the animals' movements, their eating habits, and how they interact with each other. The study of zoology is a branch of biology that involves the scientific study of animals and all aspects of animal life. The science of zoology focuses on the structure, function, and behavior, as well as the total evolution, of animals. In this section, we will take a look at how animals interact in our environment.

Lessons

Bird Food Necklace

Purpose: To make a peanut bird feeder.

Time: 10 minutes

What You'll Need: thick string about 12–15 inches long, thick needle, peanuts in the shell, whole unsalted nuts, tree or other hanging area

What to Do:
1. Tie a knot to the end of the string.
2. Use the needle to make a hole through the nuts.
3. Use the needle to push the string through the nuts, alternating the different types of nut.
4. Leave about 6–8 inches empty at the end of the string.
5. Hang up your bird feeder in an open area.
6. (Optional) Make a necklace with different type of unsalted foods.

Explanation: Many types of birds will enjoy your nutty treat. Birds quickly learn to peck the husk off the peanuts. Never feed birds with salted nuts because it can make them sick.

Dem' Bones

Purpose: To illustrate the importance of minerals in bones.

Time: 10 minutes, plus wait time

What You'll Need: uncooked chicken bone, cup of vinegar, glass jar

What to Do:
1. Remove all of the meat from an uncooked chicken bone.
2. Wash the bone in water and dry it.
3. Feel the bone and gently try to bend it.
4. Fill the jar about halfway with vinegar.
5. Place the clean bone in the vinegar and allow it to sit for about several days.
6. Remove the bone, wash it with water, and dry it.
7. Feel the bone and gently try to bend it.
8. (Optional) Repeat this experiment with other animal bones such as a steak or pork bone.

Explanation: The vinegar, which is a weak acid, dissolved the minerals in the chicken bone. This was a chemical reaction. Foods containing minerals such as calcium will keep bones strong and healthy. Without certain mineral elements, skeletons could not support the weight of the surrounding skin, muscle, and internal organs.

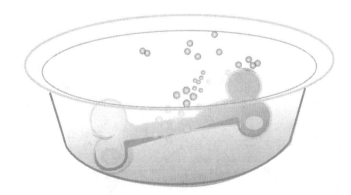

Do You Have the Backbone for This?

Purpose: To model a vertebrate animal.

Time: 1 minute

What You'll Need: umbrella

What to Do:
1. Open the umbrella and turn it upside down and examine how it is made.
2. Fold the umbrella back up and watch how the braces and ribs collapse against the central pole.

Explanation: The backbones of all vertebrate animals are an important structure in holding the ribs in place. If you could see inside an animal, you would notice a backbone and rib structure somewhat similar to the umbrella. All animals, including humans, have a backbone, or a spinal column. Fish were the first vertebrates to appear on Earth. Other vertebrates include amphibians, such as frogs; and reptiles, such as snakes; as well as birds and mammals.

Everything Is Just Ducky

Purpose: To show how ducks' feathers are waterproof.

Time: 5 minutes

What You'll Need: vegetable oil, glass of water, construction paper, scissors

What to Do:
1. Use the construction paper to draw and cut out two feathers.
2. Dip one of the feathers in the glass for a few seconds, and then remove it.
3. Coat the other feather completely with vegetable oil. Dip it in the glass for a few seconds, and then remove it.

Explanation: The water immediately absorbed the uncoated feather, but the water did not penetrate the coated feather. A bird's or duck's feather behaves much the same way as the oil-coated feather. This natural waterproofing keeps these feathered animals dry and warm.

Goldfish Breath

Purpose: To determine the breathing rate of a goldfish in different environments.

Time: 5 minutes, plus wait time

What You'll Need: a goldfish, 2 goldfish bowls or large jars, net, watch, refrigerator, sun or desk lamp with a bright bulb

What to Do:
1. Fill the two goldfish bowls with water.
2. Place one bowl in the refrigerator for about 45 minutes.
3. Place the other bowl in the sun for the same amount of time.
4. Remove the bowl from the refrigerator and place one goldfish in it.
5. Count the number of times the gills move in 2 minutes.
6. Remove the goldfish and place it in the bowl that was in the sun.
7. Repeat Step 5.

Explanation: Fish use their gills to get oxygen. There is less oxygen in warm water than there is in cold water. That is why you counted less gill movement in the colder water. In order to get the same amount of oxygen, the fish must breathe faster. When lake water gets too warm, many fish die because they cannot get enough oxygen.

Hungry Woodpecker

Purpose: To model a woodpecker's unique adaptation for gathering food.

Time: 5 minutes

What You'll Need: large raisin cookie, plate, pen, and toothpick

Safety: Do not eat the cookie after you have placed the pen in it.

What to Do:
1. Place the cookie on the plate.
2. Use the pointed end of the pen to dig out the parts of the cookie around the raisins.
3. Use the toothpick to spear the raisins and remove them from the cookie.

Explanation: The pen's point breaks away pieces of the cookie from around the raisin. The toothpick easily sticks into the raisin, allowing it to be removed. The pen models the strong bill of the woodpecker, while the toothpick models its lance-like tongue. These two features are special adaptations of the woodpecker.

Mystery Soil

Purpose: To locate animal life in different soil environments.

Time: 10 minutes

What You'll Need: soil from a sunny area, soil from a shady area, small shovel, 2 sheets of newspaper, pencil

What to Do:
1. Scoop up a small amount of soil from a sunny area and spread it out on a sheet of newspaper.
2. Try to dig down about 3–5 inches.
3. Do the same with the soil from a shady area.
4. Use your pencil as a probe and try to locate as many small insects and animals as possible for both soil types.

Explanation: You may have seen different types of small animals in the two types of soils. Chances are that the soil from the sunny area contained more life than from the shady area soil. Soil that has a more consistent source of energy (the sun), is usually more rich in nutrients and supports a wide variety of life.

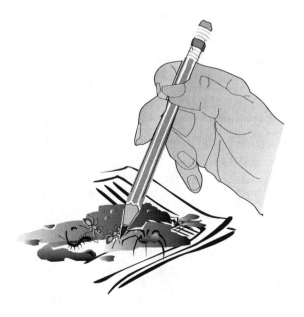

Pet Watching

Purpose: To observe characteristics about your pet.

Time: 10 minutes

What You'll Need: pet cat and/or dog, paper and pencil

What to Do:

1. Sit away from your pet and write down things you notice about it.

   For a cat watch for:
   - Tail talk: A happy cat walks with its tail held high; a frightened cat often cowers with its tail tucked between its legs.
   - Expressive faces: A curious cat will prick up its ears and open its eyes wide or twitch its whiskers; a frightened or angry cat will lay its ears back flat.
   - Playful/Learning: When cats pull things forward, like a ball of yarn, they are learning and/or being playful.
   - Cat stop: Watch where your cat goes. Most cats are creatures of habit and will have their own special lookout post and places for resting, cleaning, or sunbathing. Cats are very territorial and will rarely venture outside of their own space.

   For a dog watch for:
   - Doggie moods: As with people, you can tell a dog's mood by the expression on its face. Dogs can look questioning or fierce and can even appear to smile.
   - Nosy dogs: Notice what your dog sniffs. Their sense of smell is much better than humans.
   - Sounds: Dogs make whimpers, growls, snarls, and barks to express their needs. Can you figure out what your dog wants when he or she makes these sounds?
   - Body language: A dog shows its feelings with its whole body as well as its face. Excessive tail wagging shows excitement.

Explanation: A puppy often behaves in much the same way as a wolf cub, and kittens will play like lion cubs. You do not have to live on a farm or near a zoo to find out about animals and how they behave.

Polar Bear Parade

Purpose: To demonstrate how polar bears use fat to keep warm in the winter.

Time: 5 minutes

What You'll Need: 2 quart-sized zipper plastic bags, solid white vegetable shortening, tray of ice water, your hands

What to Do:
1. Spread about ½-inch-thick layer of the shortening on one side of the first bag. Avoid getting any of the shortening on the zip closure area.
2. Turn the second bag inside out, and put it inside the first bag so that the shortening layer is between the two bags.
3. On the side without shortening, spread another layer of shortening between the two bags.
4. Zip lock the two bags together, leaving room for your hand.
5. Place one hand in the "glove."
6. Place both hands in the tray of ice water.

Explanation: When both hands are placed in the ice water, the hand with the glove feels very warm because the protective layer of fat acts as an insulator. The solid shortening is pure fat, and fat is what protects polar bears in cold climates from the frigid climate and icy arctic waters.

See Shells by the Seashore

Purpose: To observe the homes of shelled animals.

Time: 10 minutes

What You'll Need: several different types of sea shells, coarse sandpaper

Safety: Be careful not to scrape your knuckles when rubbing the shells.

What to Do:
1. Hold the shell against a piece of sandpaper and rub it back and forth.
2. Continue until you rub right through the shell.
3. Observe what happens.

Explanation: You see a spiral chamber where the shell's inhabitants lived. These various layers are made of calcium, much like your own bones. Shells are portable homes made by animals such as cockles and snails. Some shells are shaped like saucers, while others are wound up in a tight spiral.

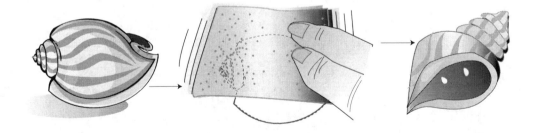

The Eyes Have It

Purpose: To model the compound vision of a grasshopper.

Time: 5 minutes

What You'll Need: 25–30 straws, moving fan, tape

What to Do:
1. Stand the straws upright and secure several strips of tape around them to make one large tube.
2. Close one eye and look through one end of the straw at a stationary object.
3. Now look at a moving fan.
4. (Optional) Make a second straw eye and keep both eyes open.

Explanation: Grasshoppers have two large eyes called compound eyes, one on each side of its head. The eyes are made up of thousands of separate units called ommatidia, and the surface of each lens is called a facet. We really do not know for sure how insects see, but your straw model might give you an example on how certain insects' sight is different from ours.

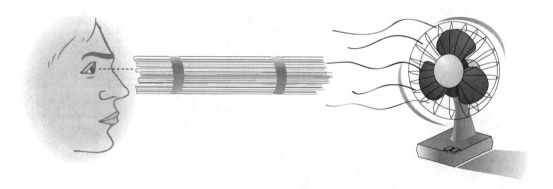

Webbing Through the Water

Purpose: To illustrate how webbed feet make it easier to swim.

Time: 5 minutes

What You'll Need: large pail or sink full of water, plastic sandwich bag, rubber band

What to Do:
1. Fill the sink full of water.
2. Spread your fingers and put your hand into the water just far enough so that only your fingers are underwater.
3. Drag your fingers back and forth through the water.
4. Take your hand out of the water and dry it.
5. Place the bag over your hand. Secure it around your wrist with the rubber band.
6. Repeat Steps 2 and 3.

Explanation: You were able to push away much more water with the bag, or webbing, than without. Frogs and toads are able to tread more water because they all have webbed feet that allow a more rapid movement in their water environment.

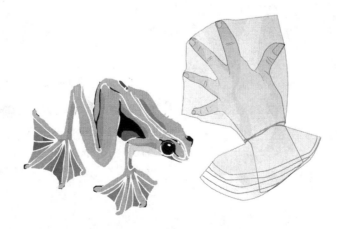

Thumbs Up

Purpose: To demonstrate the usefulness of a thumb.

Time: 5 minutes

What You'll Need: masking tape, pencil, your hand

What to Do:
1. Tape the thumb of your writing hand to your palm so that you cannot move your thumb. The tape should keep your thumb from moving but allow your other fingers to move.
2. Pick up a pencil with the taped hand and try to write your name.
3. For the next several minutes, use your taped hand to do other simple tasks such as picking up a book, turning a page, and tying your shoes.
4. Remove the tape and repeat all of the activities.

Explanation: You most likely found that doing simple tasks are very difficult with the taped thumb. Humans, chimpanzees, and gorillas all have thumbs that can touch the other four fingers. The thumb is an integral part of our bodies.

Chapter 4

Hands-On Earth Science Using Multiple Intelligences

Statistics indicate that there is very little correlation between success in life and on the job, and grades in school. Not all inventors, scientific theorists, entertainers, and presidential candidates were good students in school. Often, these are the students who harbor bad feelings about school because their strengths were not recognized.

School districts say, "All students can learn." The community says, "Teachers should be accountable for student progress and their salaries should match their performance." Teachers ask, "How can I teach all students?" Some students come to school hungry or worry about getting shot by a gang walking to school. Some students come to school having been verbally or physically abused. Some children, especially gifted students, have a great deal of ability and others have pockets of strength difficult to find. Some students come to school eager to learn and others do not see school as a priority. Teachers ask, "How can all of these students learn together in one class?"

Howard Gardner's theory of multiple intelligences addresses the issue of why successful people often are not successful in the classroom. He maintains that schools focus on too narrow of ways to present curriculum and too narrow of ways to respond to learning. Schools cater to the linguistic student who loves to read and the logical-mathematical student who loves to use formulas to solve problems. We have to captivate the interests of the rest of our students by modeling the other intelligences and valuing their contributions. We have to allow students to respond to learning in different ways using their various intelligences and value the contribution. In this way, we will reach those students who function outside the box provided by traditional teaching methods.

Obviously, teaching gifted students with multiple intelligences should not be a hit-or-miss proposition. It is not very effective if used only once in a while. It also is not very useful if it keeps us from delivering a developmentally sound, sequential set of challenging concepts. It is ineffective if we don't know how to set it up or how to evaluate it.

It is my intent to provide science content that is developmentally sound, sequential in presentation of concepts, and content rich. We will examine the Earth science topic of rocks and minerals on our planet. Many geological concepts will offer varied student responses—and that is a good thing. In addition, I will suggest time frames and realistic assessments. Hopefully, this chapter will make it possible to reach more gifted children in your class, validate their areas of strength, and work on their weaknesses, while teaching hands-on science.

Each Earth science lesson of rocks and minerals includes a simple-to-understand opening paragraph on how the hands-on science activity reinforces that particular multiple intelligence. In order to develop the big curriculum picture, it is suggested that students do all of the lessons. Each activity will follow the format below:

- **Purpose:** A brief overview of the specific type of interactive activity your students are about to experience.
- **Time:** Time is given in class periods. Each class period is considered to be approximately 40–50 minutes in length.
- **What You'll Need:** Supplies needed to complete the lab investigation. Students will need access to the Internet.

- **What to Do:** A step-by-step listing of how students are to perform each activity.

MULTIPLE INTELLIGENCES AND HOW THEY CAN BE USED

- *Verbal/Linguistic*—Learns by listening, reading, speaking, or writing (e.g., playing word games or participating in a book discussion group).
- *Logical/Mathematic*—Learns by abstracting, reasoning, categorizing, or hypothesizing (e.g., playing deduction games such as Clue).
- *Visual/Spatial*—Learns by seeing, imagining, drawing, or picturing (e.g., diagramming the human body or visiting an art museum).
- *Bodily/Kinesthetic*—Learns by touching, moving, feeling, building, or categorizing (e.g., playing Charades or taking up a new hobby).
- *Musical/Rhythmic*—Learns by singing, humming, or drumming (e.g., joining a choir or writing music).
- *Interpersonal*—Learns by relating, cooperating, teaching, and empathizing (e.g., becoming a tutor).
- *Intrapersonal*—Learns by pondering, planning, individualizing, and choosing (e.g., learning to meditate).
- *Naturalistic*—Learns by recognizing and classifying species (e.g., collecting and classifying leaves).

Verbal/Linguistic

The verbal/linguistic area has to do with words, spoken or written. Gifted students with high verbal-linguistic intelligence display a facility with words and languages. They typically are good at reading, writing, telling stories, and memorizing words along with dates. They tend to learn best by reading, taking notes, listening to lectures, and participating in discussion and debate. They also are frequently skilled at explaining, teaching, and oration or persuasive speaking. Those with verbal-linguistic intelligence learn foreign languages very easily, as they have high verbal memory and recall and an ability to understand and manipulate syntax and structure. This intelligence is highest in writers, lawyers, philosophers, journalists, politicians, and teachers.

In this lesson, students are asked to demonstrate their strengths in linguistic ability by clearly communicating scientific theory. Directions in this activity give students opportunities to provide an accurate description of a diagram of the rock cycle from a reference; to show sensitivity to subtle meanings of words by aptly distinguishing characteristics of each cycle; to include facts, records, artifacts, and references to expert scientists that support the underlying scientific concepts; and to use metaphors to help others visualize concepts.

Purpose: Students are directed to do some general scientific research on the rock cycle using the Internet or reference materials.

Time: 1–10 class periods; this can vary depending on student/teacher interest and available computer usage.

What You'll Need: Internet access and/or reference materials on the rock cycle and rocks and minerals

What to Do: Students should browse their reference materials and/ or use the Internet to Google several key Earth science terms such as: igneous rocks, sedimentary rocks, metamorphic rocks, the rock cycle, properties of minerals, how minerals form, and mineral resources. Once they have a basic understanding of these terms, students will write a creative story about what it would be like if they were able to invent a time machine and go back into that time period to observe these formations. In addition, they could draw detailed, colorful pictures of what they might observe.

Logical/Mathematical

The logical/mathematical area has to do with logic, abstractions, reasoning, and numbers. Although it often is assumed that gifted students with this intelligence naturally excel in mathematics, chess, computer programming, and other logical or numerical activities, a more accurate definition places emphasis on traditional mathematical ability, reasoning capability, abstract patterns of recognition, scientific thinking and investigation, and the ability to perform complex calculations. It correlates strongly with traditional concepts of intelligence or IQ. Many scientists, mathematicians, engineers, doctors, and economists are strongest in this area.

In this lesson, students are asked to demonstrate strength in mathematics and logic by explaining the relationship among mass, volume, and density (Density = mass/volume) and giving evidence to the validity of the formula. This can be done by making up artificial data for mass and volume and doing the various calculations. Students can design a chart for findings indicating a pattern. In assessing this activity, the teacher should be looking for accurate definitions and details, sound logical reasoning, and only necessary assumptions.

Purpose: Students will do a density lab on minerals during which they measure the mass and volume of various samples and calculate the density. This data will then be used in the next activity for classification.

Time: 2 class periods

What You'll Need: 15 mineral samples, 100-mL graduated cylinder, balance scale, water

What to Do: Students should follow this procedure for *each* mineral sample:
1. Fill the cylinder to the 50-mL mark with water.
2. Gently drop the mineral sample into the water. Do not splash.
3. Measure the new water level.
4. Subtract the two numbers (Column B – A) and record it in the Volume column (C) in the Mineral Data Table.
5. Dry the sample and place it on the balance. Record the mass to the nearest gram. Place the result in the Mass column (D) in the Mineral Data Table.
6. Divide the Mass (D) over the Volume (C) to calculate the density (D/C) of the sample.

MINERAL DATA TABLE

Mineral Name	A. Starting Volume (mL)	B. Ending Volume (mL)	C. Volume (mL) (B-A)	D. Mass (grams)	E. Density (grams/mL) (D/C)
	50				
	50				
	50				
	50				
	50				
	50				
	50				
	50				
	50				
	50				

Visual/Spatial

The visual/spatial area has to do with vision and spatial judgment. Gifted students with strong visual-spatial intelligence typically are very good at visualizing and mentally manipulating objects. Those with strong spatial intelligence often are proficient at solving puzzles. They have a strong visual memory and may be artistically inclined. Those with visual-spatial intelligence generally have a very good sense of direction and may have very good hand-eye coordination, although this is normally seen as a characteristic of the bodily-kinesthetic intelligence.

Some critics point out the high correlation between the spatial and mathematical abilities, which seems to disprove the clear separation of the intelligences as Gardner theorized. Because solving a mathematical problem involves manipulating symbols and numbers, spatial intelligence is involved in visually changing the reality. A thorough understanding of the two intelligences precludes this criticism, however, as the two intelligences do not precisely conform to the definitions of visual and mathematical abilities. Although they may share certain characteristics, they are easily distinguished by several factors, and there are visual-spatial learners with strong logical-mathematical intelligence. Careers that suit those with this intelligence include art, engineering, and architecture.

In this lesson, students will demonstrate spatial abilities by sorting like objects according to a classification key.

Purpose: Students will use an identification/classification key to identify physical characteristics and determine the specific names/identity of minerals.

Time: 2–3 class periods

What You'll Need: 15 mineral samples, glass baby food jar, sample pictures of luster and cleavage, Mineral Identification Lab Sheets 1 and 2

What to Do: Students should use the Mineral Identification Lab Sheet 1 to record their data. Using Mineral Identification Lab Sheet 2, they should follow this procedure for *each* mineral sample:
1. Determine if your sample has a metallic luster or a nonmetallic luster by looking at the example pictures. Using Lab Sheet 2, follow the arrow down to the next horizontal line, then proceed to Step 2 below.

2. Determine if the sample is softer or harder than glass by firmly holding a baby food jar and scratching the surface with the mineral sample. If you see a scratch, the sample is harder than glass; if there is not a scratch, it is softer. Check carefully for the scratch, as sometimes flakes are left behind; this is *not* a scratch. Using Lab Sheet 2, follow the arrow down to the next horizontal line, then proceed to Step 3 below.

3. Determine if the sample has cleavage (yes or no) by observing the sample pictures. The flat surfaces that appear when a mineral cracks or breaks are called cleavage. Using Lab Sheet 2, follow the arrow down to the next horizontal line, then proceed to Step 4 below.

4. Observe the color of the mineral sample.

5. Record all of your data on Lab Sheet 1.

You may want your students to visit the Mineralogical Society of America's website (http://www.minsocam.org), which contains a link to the Mineralogy 4 Kids site. This "Rock'n Internet Site" is a great place for your gifted students to learn about rocks and minerals. This site was created by a grant from the National Science Foundation for the Mineralogical Society of America and was selected by Science Educators for SciLinks. Web pages selected for SciLinks are among the best found on the Internet. It was identified only after going through a rigorous process to ensure that its content is accurate and especially useful to teachers and students. One of the first site to click on should be "Mineralogy for Kids." If your students have specific questions, they can click on "Ask a Mineralogist."

MINERAL IDENTIFICATION LAB SHEET 1

Mineral Number	Luster	Glass Test	Cleavage	Color	Mineral Name
1	N M	H S	N C		
2	N M	H S	N C		
3	N M	H S	N C		
4	N M	H S	N C		
5	N M	H S	N C		
6	N M	H S	N C		
7	N M	H S	N C		
8	N M	H S	N C		
9	N M	H S	N C		
10	N M	H S	N C		
11	N M	H S	N C		
12	N M	H S	N C		
13	N M	H S	N C		
14	N M	H S	N C		
15	N M	H S	N C		

Code:
M = metallic; N = nonmetallic; H = harder; S = softer; C = cleavage; N = no cleavage

MINERAL IDENTIFICATION LAB SHEET 2

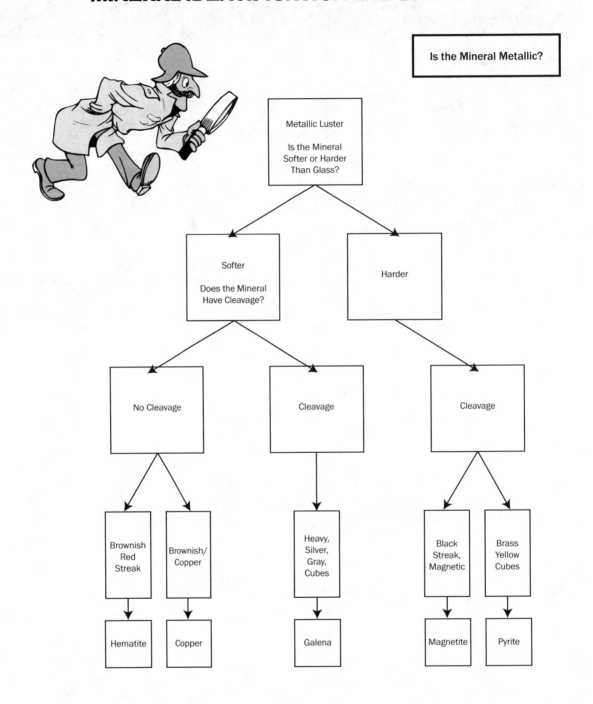

Is the Mineral Metallic?

Metallic Luster

Is the Mineral Softer or Harder Than Glass?

Softer

Does the Mineral Have Cleavage?

Harder

No Cleavage

Cleavage

Cleavage

Brownish Red Streak

Brownish/ Copper

Heavy, Silver, Gray, Cubes

Black Streak, Magnetic

Brass Yellow Cubes

Hematite

Copper

Galena

Magnetite

Pyrite

MINERAL IDENTIFICATION LAB SHEET 2

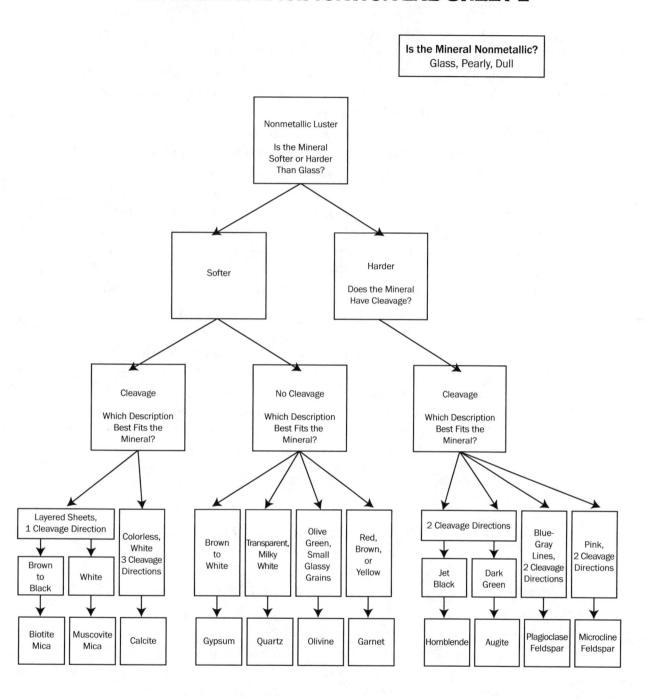

Is the Mineral Nonmetallic?
Glass, Pearly, Dull

Nonmetallic Luster

Is the Mineral Softer or Harder Than Glass?

Softer

Harder

Does the Mineral Have Cleavage?

Cleavage

Which Description Best Fits the Mineral?

No Cleavage

Which Description Best Fits the Mineral?

Cleavage

Which Description Best Fits the Mineral?

Layered Sheets, 1 Cleavage Direction

Colorless, White 3 Cleavage Directions

Brown to White

Transparent, Milky White

Olive Green, Small Glassy Grains

Red, Brown, or Yellow

2 Cleavage Directions

Blue-Gray Lines, 2 Cleavage Directions

Pink, 2 Cleavage Directions

Brown to Black

White

Jet Black

Dark Green

Biotite Mica

Muscovite Mica

Calcite

Gypsum

Quartz

Olivine

Garnet

Hornblende

Augite

Plagioclase Feldspar

Microcline Feldspar

Bodily/Kinesthetic

The bodily/kinesthetic area has to do with bodily movement. Gifted students who have this intelligence usually learn better by getting up and moving around and generally excel at physical activities such as sports or dance. They may enjoy acting or performing and usually are good at building and making things. They often learn best by doing something physically, rather than reading or hearing about it. Those with strong bodily-kinesthetic intelligence seem to use what might be termed *muscle memory*: They remember things through their body such as verbal memory or images. These students use their memorization of dance and/or musical performance extremely well and can express themselves through the creation of objects such as in engineering or craft making. Athletes, dancers, actors, surgeons, doctors, builders, and soldiers often are among those with this intelligence.

In this lesson, students demonstrate their skills in manipulating physical objects to create a sense of order (classification). Students should be encouraged to make a game so that others can mimic their process for identification. Students also might be allowed to create their own display for classification.

Purpose: Students will manipulate and use an identification/classification key to identify physical characteristics that in turn identify the three types of rocks: igneous, sedimentary, and metamorphic.

Time: 2–3 class periods

What You'll Need: 15 rock samples, Rock Identification Lab Sheets 1 and 2

What to Do: Students should use Rock Identification Lab Sheets 1 and 2 and follow this procedure for *each* rock sample:
1. Work with each sample separately.
2. Always start with the first question for each sample. Follow the instructions for each question.
3. If your rock fits the description of any of the items that are in bold, then you have determined that rock family.
4. For additional assistance, see the example pictures for types of minerals, minerals arranged in stripes, and thin flat sheets.
5. Each rock is one of three families: igneous, sedimentary, or metamorphic.

ROCK IDENTIFICATION LAB SHEET 1

1. Is the rock made of visible minerals? If YES, it cannot be SEDIMENTARY. If NO, go to 7.

2. Are the minerals of the same kind (e.g., same color, about the same shape and same hardness)? If YES, it cannot be IGNEOUS, go to 3. If NO, go to 4.

3. **A rock with crystals of the same kind is METAMORPHIC.**

4. Are the minerals of the different types evenly mixed together? If YES, go to 5. If NO, go to 6.

5. **A rock with different types of minerals evenly mixed together is IGNEOUS.**

6. **A rock with different types of minerals arranged in stripes or bands is METAMORPHIC.**

7. Is the rock frothy (full of small holes)? If YES, go to 8. If NO go to 9.

8. **A rock with lots of small holes that looks as though it has been full of gas at some time is IGNEOUS.**

9. Is the rock glassy, like a piece of colored broken glass? If YES, go to 10. If NO go to 11.

10. **A dark, hard rock that looks like glass is probably IGNEOUS formed by fast cooling of lava flow from a volcano.**

11. Is the rock made up of strong, flat sheets that look as though they split off into slate-like pieces? If YES, go to 12. If NO, go to 13.

12. **A rock that splits easily into thin, flat sheets is probably METAMORPHIC, caused by pressure.**

13. Does the rock contain easily recognized particles, like fine salt, sand, or pebbles, cemented together? If YES, go to 14. If NO, go to 15.

14. **A rock may have fossils and you may see the layering. It is SEDIMENTARY.**

15. If you have come this far, and have no answer, try it again from the top. The sample is not IGNEOUS; however, it may be SEDIMENTARY or METAMORPHIC. Some may call this a "Leaverite"; that is, "leave 'er right there and try again!"

EXAMPLES OF ROCK TYPES

Igneous Rocks

Sedimentary Rocks

Metamorphic Rocks

ROCK IDENTIFICATION LAB SHEET 2

Rock Number	Rock Family	List Three Characteristics	Rock Name
1	I S M		
2	I S M		
3	I S M		
4	I S M		
5	I S M		
6	I S M		
7	I S M		
8	I S M		
9	I S M		
10	I S M		
11	I S M		
12	I S M		
13	I S M		
14	I S M		
15	I S M		

Code:
I = igneous; M = metamorphic; S = sedimentary

Musical/Rhythmic

The musical/rhythmic area has to do with rhythm, music, and hearing. Gifted students who have a high level of musical-rhythmic intelligence display greater sensitivity to sounds, rhythms, tones, and music. They normally have good pitch (some may have absolute pitch) and are able to sing, play musical instruments, and compose music. Because there is a strong auditory component to this intelligence, those who are strongest in it may learn best via lecture. In addition, they often will use songs or rhythms to learn and memorize information and may work best with music playing in the background. Careers that suit those with this intelligence include instrumentalists, singers, conductors, disc jockeys, and composers.

This activity affords the opportunity for students with musical ability to demonstrate their originality, performance skills, rhythm, and emotional connection to the content. Although students can pick a musical composer to emulate, some students might opt to write and perform an original work. It is a good idea to have students look at various types of music. For instance, students might listen to Native American music to connect with the spirituality of the environment or the rhythm of the Earth.

Purpose: Students will write and perform their own rap or song based upon the data and information they have collected using the other intelligences.

Time: 1–2 class periods, plus some research time

What You'll Need: a creative mind, Internet access to Google song lyrics

What to Do: Students should pick their favorite musical artist and obtain a copy of one of the musician's songs (students typically can locate the lyrics on the Internet or CD liner notes). Make sure the song contains no parental advisory warning labels. Using terms from this rock and mineral unit, students should revise the song, substituting the actual lyrics with new lyrics. Allow students to use instruments and perform the new song live in front of class, should they feel comfortable doing so. If students would prefer to write their own songs instead of using preestablished music, encourage them to do so.

Interpersonal

The interpersonal area has to do with interaction with others. Gifted students who have a high interpersonal intelligence tend to be extroverts, characterized by their sensitivity to others' moods, feelings, temperaments, and motivations, as well as their ability to cooperate in order to work as part of a group. They communicate effectively and empathize easily with others, and may be either leaders or followers. They typically learn best by working with others and often enjoy discussion and debate. Careers that suit those with this intelligence include politicians, managers, teachers, and social workers.

This activity requires students to demonstrate their ability to understand and relate to others. The group process will require the individual student to share his or her learning experiences from this chapter of Earth science work and to problem solve (in the case of an answer discrepancy). A student should be assessed on his or her effort and effectiveness in problem solving and the respect shown to group members.

Purpose: Students will compare their rock and mineral classification data and results with their classmates. Class data can be graphed.

Time: 1 class period

What You'll Need: paper and pencil, plus the Rock Identification Lab Sheet 2

What to Do: Students should share their responses to the Rock Identification Lab Sheet 2. Have students compare their answer for each sample with all of their classmates. The class should come to a consensus as to the correct answers and the teacher can validate them. Record individual data on a sheet of paper. For each sample, have students draw a bar graph to record the number correct for the entire class. (It is often fun to make a contest out of the results. That is, whoever gets the most correct gets to bring a spare sample of the rock and/or mineral home as a special gift or something of the like.)

Intrapersonal

The intrapersonal area has to do with introspective and self-reflective capacities. Gifted students who are strongest in this intelligence typically are introverts and prefer to work alone. They are highly self-aware and capable of understanding their own emotions, goals, and motivations. They often have an affinity for thought-based pursuits such as philosophy. These types of students learn best when allowed to concentrate on the subject by themselves. There usually is a high level of perfectionism associated with this intelligence. Careers that suit those with this intelligence include philosophers, psychologists, theologians, writers, and scientists.

This activity allows a student to use his or her own experiences to relate to the material. The student's list can be recorded in a log or a journal. It is suggested that the student self-assess his or her work using the Student Reflection Form found in Chapter 2.

Purpose: Students will use their personal experiences to develop a list of how and where their rock and mineral samples are used in their everyday lives.

Time: 2–3 class periods

What You'll Need: reference book on rocks and minerals and/or various Internet sites, a journal or log to record data

What to Do: Students should follow the procedure below:
1. Make a list of the names of all of the rock and minerals that you knew prior to the of start this unit. Next to each one, list one or more of their uses in everyday life and give an example on how this rock or mineral makes this world a better place to live.
2. Create a second list and follow the same procedure as above for new rocks and minerals that you learned about in this unit.

Naturalist

The naturalist area has to do with nature, nurturing, and relating information to one's natural surroundings. This type of intelligence was not part of Gardner's original theory of multiple intelligences, but was added to the theory in 1996. Gifted students with this type of intelligence are said to have greater sensitivity to nature and their place within it, the ability to nurture and grow things, and greater ease in caring for, taming, and interacting with animals. They also may be able to discern changes in weather or similar fluctuations in their natural surroundings. They are good at recognizing and classifying different species. Naturalists learn best when the subject involves collecting and analyzing or is closely related to something prominent in nature. They also don't enjoy learning unfamiliar or seemingly useless subjects with few or no connections to nature. Naturalistic learners learn through being outside or in a kinesthetic way. The theory behind this intelligence often is criticized, much like the spiritual or existential intelligence, as it is seen by many as not indicative of intelligence but rather an interest. Careers that suit those with this intelligence include scientists, naturalists, conservationists, gardeners, and farmers.

This activity stretches the innate ability of the student to discover, recognize, and name various minerals and rocks found in his or her environment. The student continues the development of this intelligence by classifying these objects in their proper geological sequential order. This allows students to develop orderly thinking skills that are used every day in the real world.

Purpose: Students will take a personalized field trip around their home, neighborhood, park, or local area to collect and identify rock and mineral samples. These identified samples can be placed on a display board and classified into different categories.

Time: 1 class period

What You'll Need: outdoors, display board, tape/adhesive to display the samples

What to Do: Students should collect rock and mineral samples from the area designated by the teacher. Students should try to identify as many as possible using the knowledge they've learned in this unit. After identifying them, they should classify them according to the rock cycle order and place them on a display board.

SUGGESTED RESOURCES

Howard Gardner's Website
http://www.howardgardner.com

Gardner, H. (1983). *Frames of mind: The theory of multiple intelligences.* New York, NY: Basic Books.
Gardner, H. (1993). *Multiple intelligences: The theory in practice.* New York, NY: Basic Books.
Gardner, H. (1998). A reply to Perry D. Klein's "Multiplying the problems of intelligence by eight." *Canadian Journal of Education, 23,* 96–102.

Gardner, H. (1999). *Intelligence reframed: Multiple intelligences for the 21st century.* New York, NY: Basic Books.

Gardner, H. (2004). *Changing minds: The art and science of changing our own and other people's minds.* Boston, MA: Harvard Business School Press.

Gardner, H. (2006). *Multiple intelligences: New horizons.* New York, NY: Basic Books.

Gardner, H., & Moran, S. (2006). The science of multiple intelligences theory: A response to Lynn Waterhouse. *Educational Psychologist, 41,* 227–232.

Chapter 5

Hands-On Overhead Projector/ Document Camera Science

As professional educators, we use the overhead projector and/ or document camera in our classrooms on a daily basis. As a carpenter has his hammer and a surgeon his scalpel, we value this simple device as one of our primary tools of the trade. The importance of the overhead projector as an educational communication tool is vital to our profession. Although many of today's schools may use more high-tech tools in their classrooms, the overhead projector is still a simple, but valuable, instrument of learning. If your building no longer has an overhead projector, try picking up an inexpensive one on eBay or Craigslist. This chapter provides the opportunity for teachers to take this valuable learning tool and increase its value to an exciting new level of instruction.

On the more high-tech side, a document camera also works great. Document cameras, also known as visual presenters, digital visualizers, digital overheads, and docucams, are real-time image capture devices for displaying an object to a large audience. They are high-resolution web cams, mounted on arms so as to facilitate their placement over a page. This allows you to write on a sheet of paper or to display two- or three-dimensional objects to your students. Most document cameras also can send a video signal to a computer via USB cable. Document cameras can be connected to an interactive whiteboard (e.g., SMART Board, ActivBoard) instead of a standard screen. Many portable document cameras incorporate a flexible gooseneck design for ease of use, and some are capable of high-definition display. Most document cameras also can be supplied with an accessory so that they can be used with a microscope.

This chapter provides the opportunity for teachers to take these learning tools and increase their values to a new exciting level of instruction. For gifted students, sometimes the demonstration of a simple overhead/document camera experiment drives home a complex concept encountered in advanced courses.

I suggest you try each activity in advance before attempting them in your classroom. This will give you a good feel for the experiment you are doing, plus give you confidence with your students. You will be amazed at your students' positive reactions.

The topics in this chapter focus on the physical science, astronomy, physics, and chemistry. Each activity will follow the format below:

- **Purpose:** A brief overview of the objective of the activity and the scientific topic.
- **Time:** Estimated amount of time to perform the activity with your students.
- **What You'll Need:** A list of items that you will need to perform the activity. Most items can be obtained at your local store. Specialty items can be ordered from Flinn Scientific or another vendor.
- **Safety and Clean Up:** Special cautions and clean-up procedures, if needed, are listed here.
- **What to Do:** A step-by-step procedure on how to do the experiment.
- **Observation:** Specifics on what your students and you should observe taking place on the overhead projector/document camera.
- **Explanation:** A simple scientific reason on why you observed the results you obtained.

- **Questions for Students:** Three topic-related questions (with answers) to pose to your students about their observation. Always ask students to hypothesize or take an educated guess on what they might observe *before* you demonstrate the activity.
- **Follow-Up:** Some activities have additional experiments you can try with your students.

LESSONS

I'm Attracted to You

Purpose: To classify metal and nonmetal objects using a magnet.

Time: 5 minutes

What You'll Need: bar magnet, plastic ring, paper clip, iron nail, cardboard square, piece of wood, marble, metal square, metal screw, plastic wall anchor, any other small metal and nonmetal objects

What to Do:
1. Place all of the objects on top of the overhead.
2. Ask students to predict what will be attracted to the magnet and what will not.
3. Place the magnet on each object and slowly pull it away.

Observation: All metal objects, such as the paper clip, iron nail, and metal screw, will be attracted to the magnet. Nonmetal objects, such as the plastic ring, cardboard square, piece of wood, plastic wall anchor, and marble, will not be attracted to the magnet.

Explanation: Any metal that contains the element iron will be magnetic. A metal object made of brass or aluminum is not attracted to magnets. Magnetism is the attraction of a magnet for another object. All magnets have two ends, or poles: a North Pole and a South Pole. Poles are a pair of unlike, or opposite, charges.

Questions for Students:
1. How can you tell if an object is magnetic or not? (It moves toward the magnet if it is magnetic.)
2. What things in your home are magnetic? (Possible answers: refrigerator magnet, freezer door, TV set, computer, metal chairs)
3. What do opposite charges do? (They attract to each other.)

You Have That Magnetic Personality

Purpose: To show how a magnetic field surrounds a magnet.

Time: 10 minutes

What You'll Need: 2 bar magnets, container of iron filings

What to Do:
1. Part 1: Center one bar magnet under the overhead projector clear plastic. If you are using a document camera, place a clear piece of plastic wrap over the magnet. Gently sprinkle the filings over the magnet. Have students make a drawing of their observation.
2. Part 2: Line up two magnets under the plastic with North facing North. Gently sprinkle the filings over the magnet. Have students make a drawing of their observation.
3. Part 3: Line up two magnets under the plastic with North facing South. Gently sprinkle the filings over the magnet. Have students make a drawing of their observation.

Observation:

Part 1

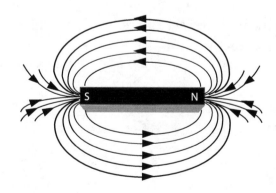

Part 2

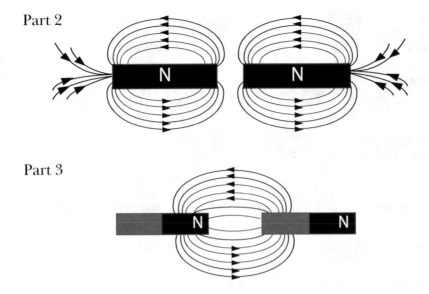

Part 3

Explanation: Magnetic forces are exerted all around a magnet, not just at the poles. The region of magnetic force around a magnet is known as a *magnetic field*. Magnetic fields allow magnets to interact without touching.

In Part 1, the lines, called magnetic field lines, map out the field around the magnet. Magnetic field lines spread out from one pole, curve around a magnet, and return to the other pole. Although you cannot actually see a magnetic field, you can see its effect. In Parts 2 and 3, when magnetic fields of two or more magnets overlap, the result is a combined field.

Questions for Students:
1. What is a magnetic pole? (The magnetic pole is the two opposite ends of a magnet.)
2. What are the magnetic poles called? (North and South Poles.)
3. How do the poles attract and repel? (Like poles repel and opposite poles attract.)

Going in Circles

Purpose: To draw conclusions on which way a compass will point in a magnetic field.

Time: 10 minutes

What You'll Need: bar magnet, compass (clear, round), overhead projector pen

What to Do:
1. Place the bar magnet under the plastic in the center of the overhead. If you are using a document camera, place a clear piece of plastic wrap over the magnet.
2. Place the compass about one inch beyond the North Pole of the magnet.
3. Draw a small arrow showing the direction of the compass needle.
4. Repeat Steps 2 and 3 one inch beyond the North Pole of the magnet. Do this about 25 times.
5. Remove the magnet and observe the pattern you drew.

Observation: The arrows form a circle around the North Pole.

Explanation: The pattern of arrows represents the magnetic field. Compasses also respond to magnetic materials near them. Earth has a gigantic magnetic field surrounding it, just like the bar magnet. Earth's magnetic field affects the movement of electrically charged particles in space. Charged particles also affect Earth's magnetic field.

Questions for Students:
1. What does the pattern of arrows represent? (It represents the magnetic field.)

2. Do compasses respond only to the Earth's magnetic field? (No. A compass also can respond to an electromagnet, such as a motor, a solenoid, heads of hard disks, tape drives, and speakers.)

3. Are magnetic fields stronger or weaker at the poles of a magnet? (Stronger. Because the Earth is fairly thick at its equator, it is difficult to detect much of any magnetic force there.)

Follow-Up: Repeat this activity with two bar magnets at different positions on the overhead.

Color Combos

Purpose: To compare how colors are combined in light.

Time: 5 minutes

What You'll Need: cellophane sheets of blue, yellow, green, and red

What to Do: After you place each sheet on top of one another, ask students to observe what they see.
1. Place the yellow cellophane sheet on top of the blue sheet.
2. Place the blue cellophane sheet on top of the red sheet.
3. Place the green cellophane sheet on top of the red sheet.
4. Place the red cellophane sheet on top of the blue sheet.
5. Place the green cellophane sheet on top of the blue sheet.
6. Place the yellow cellophane sheet on top of the blue sheet on top of the red.

Observation:

yellow + blue = green
blue + red = purple
green + red = yellow
red + blue = magenta
green + blue = cyan
green + blue + red = white

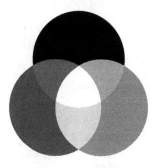

Explanation: Colors combine in different ways to make other colors. The three colors that can be combined to make any other color are called *primary colors*. They are red, green, and blue. When combined in equal amounts, the primary colors produce white light. But, if they combine in varying amounts, they can produce any other color. Yellow, cyan, and magenta are *secondary colors* because they are each produced from two primary colors. A primary color combined with a secondary color gives you a *complimentary color.*

Questions for Students:
1. Why do objects have different colors? (Objects reflect colors that are seen and absorb the other colors of light.)
2. What are the primary colors? (Red, green, and blue.)
3. What are the secondary colors? (Cyan, yellow, and magenta.)

Made in the Shade

Purpose: To illustrate how polarized filters block light.

Time: 2 minutes

What You'll Need: 2 sheets of polarized light filters (with arrows pointed up), scissors

What to Do:
1. Cut two 4–5-inch strips of polarized light filters. On top of each of the strips, cut a v-shaped point about one inch from the top.
2. Place one of the filter arrows pointing up on the overhead projector.
3. Place the second filter, arrow pointing up, next to the first.
4. Place the first lens on top of the second.
5. Turn the lens on top 90 degrees to the right.

Observation: Light shines through the filter when both arrows are pointing up. When you turn the top lens, no light is emitted from the lens combination.

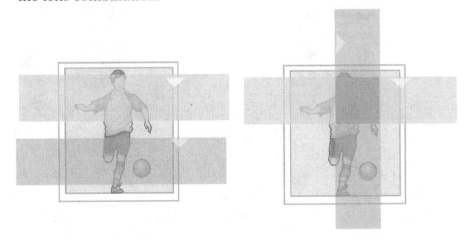

Explanation: When two polarized filters are combined at a 90-degree angle, no light can come through. Sunglasses with polarized lens filters behave the same way. When light enters a polarized filter, only some of the light waves can pass through. There are tiny slits that run either horizontal or vertical. When you turn the lenses, both get dark so you can no longer see the object.

Questions for Students:

1. How does light travel? (It travels in waves.)
2. How do you know that light is a wave? (When light enters a polarized filter, only some waves can pass through.)
3. What would happen if you took two pairs of sunglasses and placed them at a 90-degree angle with each other? (No light would pass through.)

Follow-Up: Repeat this activity with two pairs of sunglasses. Hold them up to the light and cross one lens with the other.

Wacky Science © Prufrock Press

Permission is granted to photocopy or reproduce this page for classroom use only.

111

Dissolving Seasonings

Purpose: To display how salt is soluble in water, but pepper is not.

Time: 5 minutes

What You'll Need: glass pie pan, pepper, salt, stirring rod, water

Safety and Clean Up: Flush the extra pepper down the drain.

What to Do:
1. Fill the pan with warm water.
2. Pour the salt and the pepper in the pan.
3. Stir.

Observation: The salt dissolves but the pepper will not dissolve in the water.

Explanation: A substance that does not dissolve is said to be insoluble. Pepper is insoluble, whereas salt, which will dissolve in water, is soluble.

Questions for Students:
1. Does taste play a factor in what dissolves and what does not dissolve? (No.)
2. List other common food items that will dissolve in water. (Sugar, syrup, cocoa, lemonade mix, etc.)
3. List some common food items that will not dissolve in water. (Most non-salt-type seasonings, vegetables, fruits, etc.)

Follow-Up: Repeat this activity with other common kitchen seasonings, such as turmeric, sage, rosemary, thyme, basil, cinnamon, cumin, ginger, saffron, or nutmeg, to name a few.

Day or Night?

Purpose: To identify the effects of Earth's rotation and revolution.

Time: 5 minutes

What You'll Need: globe of the Earth (plastic, inflatable)

What to Do:
1. Turn off the light and the overhead projector in the classroom.
2. Place the globe level with the Earth's equator about 3 feet from the projection lens of the overhead projector. Have your hometown facing the overhead projector.
3. Turn on the overhead projector. Notice where light is shining and what part of the globe is dark, or has a shadow.
4. Slowly turn the globe so your hometown is now on the dark side.
5. Now continue to turn the globe to where your hometown is located. When your hometown is on the lighted side, observe different locations.

Observation: Half of the globe facing the projector light will be lit and move into the shadow as the globe is rotated.

Explanation: A complete spin of the globe represents one rotation of Earth on its axis, which equals one day. As Earth rotates eastward, the sun appears to move westward across the sky. It is day on the side of the Earth facing the sun. As Earth continues to turn to the east, the sun appears to set in the west. Sunlight cannot reach the side of the Earth facing away from the sun, so it is nighttime. This whole cycle takes 24 hours.

Questions for Students:
- When the globe was rotated to our hometown, which part of the globe has the light shining upon it? (The hometown.) Which part was in the shadow? (The opposite side of the globe.)
- The overhead projector light is a model of what? (The sun.)
- What does a complete spin of the globe represent? (One day.)

Reasons for the Seasons

Purpose: To demonstrate how the revolution of the Earth affects the seasons.

Time: 5 minutes

What You'll Need: globe of the Earth (an inflatable globe works fine)

What to Do:

1. Place the top of the globe in the center of a table that you are able to walk completely around.
2. Tilt the globe about 23.5 degrees, so that the Northern Hemisphere is tilted toward the overhead projector. This represents the Earth's position at the June, or summer, solstice.
3. Walk around the overhead projector in a circle but keep the tilt the same relative to the room, not the overhead. As you walk, stop every 90 degrees to represent Earth's position at the September, or fall, equinox, and the December, or winter, solstice. Your final stop will be the March, or spring, equinox.
4. At each position, ask students to describe the seasonal conditions in the United States.

Observation: Your four stops are:

- Position 1 (summer solstice): The north end of the Earth's axis is tilted toward the overhead (sun). It is summer in the Northern Hemisphere and winter in the Southern Hemisphere.
- Position 2 (fall equinox): Neither end of the Earth's axis is tilted toward the sun. Both hemispheres receive the same amount of energy.
- Position 3 (winter solstice): The south end of Earth's axis is tilted toward the sun. It is summer in the Southern Hemisphere and winter in the Northern Hemisphere.
- Position 2 (spring equinox): Neither end of the Earth's axis is tilted toward the sun. Both hemispheres receive the same amount of energy.

Explanation: Most places outside the tropics have four distinct seasons: winter, spring, summer, and fall. The Earth has seasons because its axis is tilted as it moves around the sun. The Earth has 23.5-degree tilt at all times. A solstice is a day when the noon sun is overhead 23.5 degrees north or south. This occurs when one end of the Earth's axis is tilted most directly toward the sun. The term equinox means equal night and occurs when neither pole of Earth's axis is titled toward the sun.

Questions for Students:

1. Why is it colder at the poles compared to the equator? (There is less sun to warm the Earth.)
2. What is the difference between rotation and revolution? (Rotation is turning around the axis; revolution is movement around another object.)
3. What is the process that causes day and night? (Earth rotates on its axis once a day. As it rotates, half of the Earth's surface faces the sun [day] and half of the Earth's surface faces away from the sun [night]).

Eclipsing Situation

Purpose: To differentiate between a solar and a lunar eclipse.

Time: 5 minutes

What You'll Need: globe of the Earth (an inflatable globe works fine), Styrofoam (or rubber) ball

What to Do:
1. Darken the room and turn on the overhead.
2. Place the globe in the center of the overhead.
3. To model a lunar eclipse, place the Styrofoam ball a few inches above the globe and notice the shadow on the ceiling.
4. To model a solar eclipse, remove the globe, and place the ball on the center of the overhead. Hold the globe a few inches above the ball. Notice the shadow on the Earth.

Observation: A lunar eclipse has no light when it reaches the moon, whereas a solar eclipse displays a round shadow that forms on the globe.

Lunar   Solar

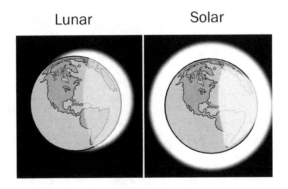

Explanation: When the shadow of the moon hits our planet Earth, an eclipse occurs. A solar eclipse occurs when the moon passes between the Earth and the sun, blocking the sunlight from reaching the Earth. A lunar eclipse occurs at a full moon when Earth is directly between the moon and the sun.

Questions for Students:
- What is a full moon? (One is able to see the whole lighted side of the moon. This is the only time when the Earth is between the sun and moon and therefore in a position to completely block the light from the sun.)
- Why do lunar eclipses occur only at full moon? (A full moon is the only time that the light from the sun is completely blocked.)
- What is a partial eclipse? (When the moon, sun, and Earth are not in line.)

Colorful Crystals

Purpose: To observe crystal formation.

Time: 10 minutes, plus 1 day wait time

What You'll Need: glass pie plate, several charcoal briskets, table salt, ammonia, liquid bluing, food coloring (not red), measuring cup, mixing bowl, spoon, water

Safety and Clean Up: Use caution when working with ammonia and bluing. Do not breathe the ammonia. After observation, crystals can be trashed.

What to Do:
1. Place the pie plate on the overhead projector.
2. Place enough charcoal in the plate to cover the bottom.
3. Mix the following in the mixing bowl and stir:
   - ¼ cup water
   - ½ cup of ammonia
   - ¼ cup liquid bluing
   - ¼ cup of table salt

4. Carefully pour the mixture over the charcoal, making sure all of the pieces get wet.
5. In random order, squirt a few drops of food coloring in the charcoal.
6. Set aside the pan in an undisturbed place for one day and then observe the results.

Observation: A colorful growth of crystal appears on the plate.

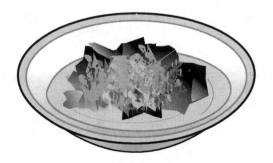

Explanation: Your crystal garden is an actual recrystallization of the table salt. The chemical reaction of the bluing and ammonia breaks part of the solid charcoal into a liquid. The remaining solid charcoal soaks up all the moisture it can until it becomes super-saturated; that is, it cannot hold any more moisture. As the liquid evaporates, the salt solution begins to dry and crystallize again in a new form. The food coloring gives the crystals the unique blend of colors. This process is how minerals form crystals inside the Earth.

Questions for Students:

1. Would the crystals form if there was no charcoal? (No, because the charcoal acts as a seed, or starting point for growth.)
2. What is the purpose of the ammonia and bluing? (They assist in the chemical reaction.)
3. This is a model of what is commonly known as a geode. Geodes have long been objects of curiosity, their sparkling interiors containing some of the most beautiful crystals to be found anywhere in the world. Based upon the results of this activity, can you give a scientific definition of a geode? (A rock having a cavity lined with inward growing crystals.)

Dancing Colors

Purpose: To observe the reaction of two clear liquids to form a precipitate.

Time: 5 minutes

What You'll Need: 2 beakers, lead nitrate solution, potassium iodide solution, stirring rod

Safety and Clean Up: Use caution when working with chemicals; wear safety glasses. Do not touch chemicals. Dispose of all materials by flushing them down the drain with plenty of water.

What to Do:
1. Place both empty beakers on the overhead projector.
2. Pour equal amounts of each liquid into each beaker. Make sure each beaker is less than half full.
3. Pour one liquid into the other. Stir. Allow the precipitate to settle for several minutes.

Observation: A yellow solid, or precipitate, forms.

Explanation: A chemical reaction takes place. The formation of the yellow solid is called a precipitate. The yellow solid is called the product of this double replacement chemical reaction. It can never be reversed back to the original clear liquids.

Questions for Students:
1. What would happen if all of the liquid was allowed to evaporate? (A yellow mustard-like solid would remain.)
2. Can you ever get the two clear liquids to return to their original solutions? (No.)
3. How does a chemical change differ from a physical change? (In a chemical change, a new substance is formed; in a physical change, no new substance is formed.)

Follow-Up: Allow the liquid to evaporate for a few days and observe the results.

Orange You Happy to See Me?

Purpose: To observe the solubility rates of two solutions to form a precipitate.

Time: 5 minutes

What You'll Need: small beaker, mercuric chloride, potassium iodide, stirring rod

Safety and Clean Up: Use caution when working with chemicals; wear safety glasses. Do not touch chemicals. Dispose of all materials by flushing them down the drain with plenty of water.

What to Do:
1. Pour a few ounces of mercuric chloride into the beaker on the overhead projector.
2. Slowly pour the potassium iodide into the beaker a few drops at a time. Stir until the orange substance disappears.
3. Continue pouring the potassium iodide into the mercuric chloride until the orange material remains in the solution.

Observation: At first, the orange solution seems to magically disappear, but when you continue to add more potassium iodide, the entire solution remains the color orange.

Explanation: The two solutions combine in a chemical reaction to form a new product, which is an orange, solid precipitate. The solution returns to its original, colorless state due to the excess of potassium iodide that is soluble. Solubility is a measure of how well one liquid dissolves into another. When you pour an excess of potassium iodide into the mercuric chloride, you have a supersaturated solution, so the orange precipitate, or solid, remains.

Questions for Students:
1. Why did the orange color disappear after the first few drops were added? (It is not a saturated solution.)

2. What do we call a solid that forms from two clear liquids? (A precipitate.)
3. What is another example of something that is supersaturated? (A sponge full of water, soaking wet clothing such as a bathing suit, a grassy field after a rain storm, etc.)

Follow-Up: Allow the liquid to evaporate for a few days and observe the results.

I'm Seeing Red

Purpose: To demonstrate how color change is involved in a chemical reaction.

Time: 5 minutes

What You'll Need: resealable plastic bag, teaspoon, baking soda, calcium chloride, phenol red solution

Safety and Clean Up: Use caution when working with chemicals; wear safety glasses. Do not touch chemicals. Dispose of all materials by flushing them down the drain with plenty of water.

What to Do:
1. Add one teaspoon of baking soda to one corner of the bag.
2. Add one teaspoon of calcium chloride to the same corner of the bag.
3. Mix both materials by shaking the bag.
4. In the opposite corner, place two teaspoons of phenol red solution.
5. Seal the bag and place it on top of the overhead projector.
6. Mix the bag's contents by shaking it.

Observation: The contents of the bag turn yellow and the bag expands.

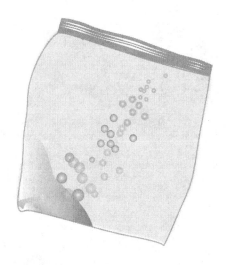

Explanation: A chemical reaction takes place when the phenol red solution mixes with the dry chemicals. The bag expands because carbon dioxide gas is released in the reaction. Phenol red is a chemical indicator that changes color in the presence of a base. A base is the opposite of an acid.

Questions for Students:
1. Why was there no reaction when the two dry chemicals were mixed? (Most reactions take place only when a liquid, like water, is present.)
2. Name other things that change colors during chemical reactions. (Leaves changing color in the autumn, decaying food, etc.)
3. Can things change colors without going through a chemical reaction? Give an example. (Yes, powdered beverages dissolving in water is one example.)

Diaper Madness

Purpose: To observe the effect of a super absorbent polymer.

Time: 10 minutes

What You'll Need: sodium polyacrylate (order from Flinn Scientific or another vendor), Petri dish, salt, stirring rod, water

Safety and Clean Up: Dump the gel into the trash. Do not get the white powder in your eyes.

What to Do:
1. Fill the dish with water and place it on top of the overhead projector.
2. Slowly add a small amount of the sodium polyacrylate to the dish and stir.
3. Sprinkle salt over the gel.

Observation: The water turns into a thick jelly-like substance. When you sprinkle salt over the gel, it will cause it to turn back to a liquid.

Explanation: The water particles go in between the sodium polyacrylate particles and turn into a soft solid, which we call a gel. This gel is a polymer—a long complex chain of molecules. This polymer absorbs about 300 to 500 times its mass in water. This is the main ingredient in baby diapers. The salt releases the pressure of the powder in between the water and turns the gel back into liquid water.

Questions for Students:
1. Why do you think this is a good product for baby's diapers? (It absorbs urine well.)
2. What would happen if you got this powder in your eye? (It would gel up the water in the eye and start to sting—like getting salt in your eye.)
3. Would the gel form quicker with warm or cold water? (Warm water because warm water particles move faster than cold water particles, therefore the rate of reaction is faster.)

Disappearing Peanuts

Purpose: To show that Styrofoam contains mostly air particles.

Time: 5 minutes, plus wait time

What You'll Need: bag of Styrofoam peanuts, acetone, glass container (not plastic), stirring rod (not plastic), waxed paper

Safety and Clean Up: Use caution when working with acetone as it is flammable and toxic. It can burn the skin. Dispose of the "melted" peanuts in the trash.

What to Do:
1. Over a sink, fill the glass container about half full of acetone and place it on the overhead projector.
2. Add one peanut and push it into the acetone.
3. Repeat this several times.
4. Carefully remove the "melted" peanuts on a clean sheet of waxed paper and allow them to harden for a few hours.
5. Pour the used acetone back into the container.
6. Observe the results.

Observation: The white peanuts seem to melt, like ice cream. When dried, they harden into the shape you placed them in on the waxed paper.

Explanation: When Styrofoam is mixed with acetone (a paint remover), the trapped gases in the peanuts escape and only a small piece of residue remains. This residue can be recovered, washed, and recycled. Because this is a physical change, not a chemical change, the acetone and the peanuts can be recycled and used again and again.

Questions for Students:
1. What would happen if you tried this with a Styrofoam cup? (The results would be the same.)

2. What can recycled Styrofoam be used for? (Park benches, car bumpers, etc.)

3. What do you recycle at your home? (Answers will vary.)

I'm Running Hot and Cold

Purpose: To observe the difference of molecular movement between hot and cold particles.

Time: 5 minutes

What You'll Need: bottles of blue and red food coloring, 2 beakers, container of hot water and cold water

What to Do:
1. Fill one beaker with hot water and the other beaker with cold water (the hotter and colder, the better).
2. Place both on top of the overhead projector.
3. Place two drops of red food coloring in the beaker with hot water.
4. Place two drops of blue food coloring in the beaker with the cold water.

Observation: The red particles spread out much faster than the blue cold-water particles.

Explanation: Substances move faster in warm particles than in cold particles. This happens because the particles, or molecules, are spread farther apart in warm solutions and have more space to move around. There is less space in between cold particles, so it is more difficult for the food coloring to move about.

Questions for Students:
1. Which type of particles moves faster? (The particles in the warm water.) Which type of particles moves slower? (The particles in the cold water.)
2. Which type of air can hold more moisture, warm air or cold air? (Warm air.)
3. What would happen with a beaker that contained a mixture of hot and cold water? (The particle movement would be in between the two observed.)

Travelin' Toothpicks

Purpose: To display surface tension movement.

Time: 5 minutes

What You'll Need: glass pie pan, 6 toothpicks, liquid soap, sugar cube, water

What to Do:
1. Fill the pan with water and place it on the overhead projector.
2. Arrange the toothpicks in a circle format on top of the water. The center of the toothpicks should all be pointing toward the center of the pan.
3. Place a sugar cube in the center of the pan.
4. Place a drop or two of the soap in the center of the pan.

Observation: The toothpicks are drawn to the center of the pan with the sugar. The soap droplets push the toothpick away from the center.

Explanation: The sugar absorbs the water, which in turn creates a small current that moves the toothpicks toward the center. The soap gives off an oily substance that breaks the surface tension on the top layer of the water. This causes the toothpicks to push outward. Surface tension is a force caused by the attraction between molecules of a liquid at its surface, giving the effect of an elastic skin on the liquid.

Questions for Students:

1. What is the purpose of dish detergent? (To break the surface tension of the water, which makes the water wetter and therefore enhances their cleaning ability.)
2. How do water spiders walk on water? (The elastic surface tension is strong enough to hold them up.)
3. What would happen if you added more drops of soap to the toothpicks? (They would sink.)

Follow-Up: Try this activity with different liquids such as club soda or milk.

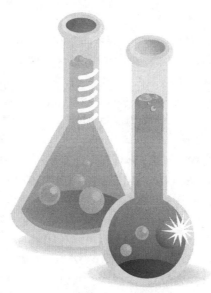

Chapter 6

Science Fair Projects Made Simple

Clearly, the top science education activity for all students, including the gifted, is the science fair project. This teaches children how scientists follow the scientific method to solve problems. There is no better way to teach complex scientific principles than to actually have students make this type of interactive commitment.

Although the science fair project is great methodology for gifted students to really expand their knowledge base and act like real scientists, sometimes the teacher may think, "Science fair—it's just not fair." Once you decide to undertake this grand endeavor, it is important to realize that this is not only a major time commitment for the student—and their parents—it is also very time consuming for you as the teacher.

The intent of this chapter is not to suggest topics or how to run your local, regional, or state science fair. There are many great resources already available that cover these issues. Instead, this chapter is a way to make the process of dealing with the mechanics of the science fair easier to understand, not just for you, but also for the students and their parents who will be actively involved in this activity. In roles as a parent, teacher, and regional and state science fair judge, I have successfully worked with science fairs for more than three decades with my elementary and middle school students. I have developed the forms included in this chapter with the input and assistance of hundreds of my educational colleagues. Although the focus of these pages is the detailed science fair content, the intent is to make the process very simple and easier to manage. Feel free to copy the forms and distribute them to your students and their parents. Each form is discussed below.

Science Fair Project Arrangement of Written Report: This form has all of the requirements of the science fair project written report. It also identifies what specific items are required on the tri-fold display board with an asterisk (*). The short explanation of each category is very helpful for students and parents.

Checklist #1: Purpose and Hypothesis, Checklist #2: Materials and Procedures, Checklist #3: Variables and Experimental Error, and Checklist #4: Results and Conclusion: These lists should be passed out as a set with the Science Fair Project Arrangement of Written Report handout stapled on top. Establish a due date for each form before you give the packet to your students. At the bottom of each form is a place for a parent/guardian signature. This step is a very important part of the process as it keeps parents informed about their child's progress. You must approve each individual form before the student moves on to the next one.

Science Fair Project Evaluation Rubric and Science Fair Project Oral Presentation Rubric: These rubrics are simple, detailed, and to the point. Feel free to share a copy of these rubrics with your students in advance so they know that there are no surprises in the evaluation method. I have always used a point system and percentage to evaluate students. Feel free to use the point system on the rubric, and then use a weight factor to fit it in with your grading system.

SCIENCE FAIR PROJECT ARRANGEMENT OF WRITTEN REPORT

Abstract*
- Place the project title in bold.
- Purpose: Explain what you set out to do.
- Procedure: Explain how you did your experiment.
- Conclusion: Explain the results you obtained.

Safety Sheet*

Title Page
The following need to be centered: project title, your name, teacher's name, school, and state or local region number.

Table of Contents
Begin numbering the Table of Contents with page 1.

Acknowledgements
This is where you thank all of the people who assisted you with your project: parents, teachers, friends, and so forth.

Purpose and Hypothesis*
Purpose is the question you plan to answer, and it is written as a single sentence (in question format). The one-sentence hypothesis is written as an if-then sentence: *If* I do this, *then* this will be the result.

Review of Literature/Research Paper With Bibliography
This section incorporates all of the important information you found in books, magazines, and other material; learned from interviews; retrieved from the Internet; and located elsewhere while researching your topic. The review of the literature needs to be in your own words. This should be typed and double-spaced. Citations are required.

Variables and Experimental Error*
- Experimental variable: What is being tested?
- Dependent variable: What is measurable?
- Controls: List all variables that stay the same or constant.
- List all errors and mistakes that could possibly be made in your experiment.

Materials*

Include a complete list of all of the materials used in the experiment. Do not number them.

Procedure*

Your procedure needs to be clear, concise, and sequential. It needs to be written so that anyone can duplicate your experiment. Number all steps.

Results*

This may include computer-generated data charts and tables, measurements, and graphs.

Conclusion*

This is a short one- or two-paragraph summary or analysis that answers the question in your purpose. You should remember to make reference to your hypothesis.

Note. The asterisk (*) indicates items that will be included on the tri-fold board.

CHECKLIST #1: PURPOSE AND HYPOTHESIS

Name: _____

Due date: _____

Project Title:

Purpose: Purpose is the question you plan to answer, and it is written as a single sentence (in question format).

Hypothesis: The one-sentence hypothesis is written as an if-then sentence: *If* I do this, *then* this will be the result.

Parent signature required: _____
(No credit given without signature.)

Do not write below this space. For teacher use only.
____ Approved, continue to next checklist page.
____ Corrections needed; see teacher for mini-conference (use backside for changes).
____ Changes approved.

CHECKLIST #2: MATERIALS AND PROCEDURE

Name: _____

Due date: _____

Project Title:

Materials: List all of the equipment/materials you will need to run the experiment. Do not number the list.

Procedure: This includes a very detailed, step-by-step listing of *everything* you are doing. Number all steps.

Parent signature required: _____
(No credit given without signature.)

Do not write below this space. For teacher use only.
    ___ Approved, continue to next checklist page.
    ___ Corrections needed; see teacher for mini-conference (use backside for changes).
    ___ Changes approved.

CHECKLIST #3: VARIABLES AND EXPERIMENTAL ERROR

Name: _____

Due date: _____

Purpose: Include your purpose below.

Experimental/Independent Variable: What are you testing?

Dependent Variable: What is being measured? Remember to use metric units.

Controls: List all factors that are not changing in your experiment.

Experimental Errors: List all possible mistakes or errors that can take place while you are running your experiment.

Parent signature required: _____
(No credit given without signature.)

Do not write below this space. For teacher use only.
   ___ Approved, continue to next checklist page.
   ___ Corrections needed; see teacher for mini-conference (use backside for changes).
   ___ Changes approved.

CHECKLIST #4: RESULTS AND CONCLUSION

Name: _____

Due date: _____

Purpose: Include your purpose below.

Results, Data, Charts, and Graphs: Attach all computer-generated data charts and tables, measurements, and graphs with a paper clip to this page.

Conclusion: This is a short one- or two-paragraph summary that answers the question in your purpose.

Parent signature required: _____
(No credit given without signature.)

Do not write below this space. For teacher use only.
   ___ Approved, continue to next checklist page.
   ___ Corrections needed; see teacher for mini-conference (use backside for changes).
   ___ Changes approved.

SCIENCE FAIR PROJECT EVALUATION RUBRIC

Purpose and Hypothesis:

(2) Purpose clearly defined and testable hypothesis.

(1) Purpose and hypothesis fairly logical.

(0) Neither the purpose nor hypothesis is clear or present.

Variables:

(5) Experimental/dependent variable clearly listed; correctly defined.

(4, 3) All present; a bit unclear.

(2) One variable correct.

(0) No variables listed/correct.

Experimental Approach:

(4) Control/comparison group present.

(3) Attempt made to control variable.

(2) Method inappropriate/attempt made.

(1) No control/comparison present.

(0) No demonstration or exhibit

Materials and Procedure:

(10, 9) Very detailed list of materials and procedure are clearly stated.

(8, 7) Detailed list of materials and procedure are stated.

(6, 5) Partial list of materials and procedure are stated.

(4, 3) Many details and specifics missing in both materials and procedure.

(2, 1) Incomplete/unclear materials or procedure.

(0) None listed.

Data/Results:

(12, 11) Excellent data; experimental error considered.

(10, 9) Good quality data; some errors.

(8, 7, 6) Fair quality; errors.

(5, 4, 3) Poor quality; unreliable; many errors.

(2, 1, 0) Unacceptable data/results.

_____ No use of metric (-2)

_____ No multiple trials (-3)

_____ No averaging (-2)

_____ Not reliable/logical (-5)

Conclusion:

(4) Correlations are drawn from data/results; valid.

(3) Conclusion is present, but not consistent with data.

(1) Inappropriate, irrelevant, invalid conclusion.

(0) None listed.

(Rubric continues on next page.)

Rubric, continued

Graphics:

(5) Excellent computer-labeled charts, graphs, pictures, and photos (two minimum).

(4) Good quality/only one included.

(3, 2) Fair quality.

(1, 0) Poor quality or no graphics.

Visual Impact/Organization:

(10, 9) Sharp, neat, orderly, organized overall appearance.

(8, 7) Above-average appearance/organization.

(6, 5) Average appearance/organization.

(4, 3) Below-average appearance/organization.

(2, 1) Poor appearance/organization.

Review of Literature/Research: (5)   (4)   (3)   (2)   (1)   (0)

Project Level of Difficulty: (3)   (2)   (1)

complex   average   simple

Total Rubric Points: _____ × weight factor _____ = _____

Score: _____ / _____ = _____ %

SCIENCE FAIR PROJECT ORAL PRESENTATION RUBRIC

I. Purpose (Project Organization)

(4) Conveys clear, focused ideas by organizing an introduction with a purpose, body, and conclusion.

(3) Presentation includes purpose and clear conclusion.

(2) Either purpose or topic is unclear.

(1) Neither the topic nor the purpose is clear.

(0) No purpose is stated.

II. Clarity (Volume)

(4) Adjusts volume for conditions to always be heard.

(3) Heard by all of the audience.

(2) Heard by some of the audience.

(1) Few audience members are able to hear.

(0) Inaudible, even after coaxing.

III. Delivery (Pronunciation)

(4) Words are pronounced correctly and understood; terms are restated and paraphrased.

(3) Words are pronounced correctly and understood.

(2) Some pronunciation errors; some interference with communication.

(1) Errors are so numerous that they interfere with communication.

(0) Not practiced.

IV. Articulation (Eye Contact, Body Movement)

(4) Maintains eye contact with the audience; gestures and body movement are adjusted for conditions preceding, during, and following the presentation.

(3) Makes eye contact with the audience; gestures and body movement match message.

(2) Only occasional eye contact; some inappropriate gestures and body movement.

(1) Poor eye contact; inappropriate gestures and body movement.

(0) No eye contact, no gestures, or body movement.

V. Response to Audience (Answers Questions)

(4) Responses always make sense, are in the form of a declarative sentence, and are consistent with question posed; can include documentation when appropriate.

(3) Responses sometimes lack necessary information; further information can be provided on request.

(2) Responses sometimes lack necessary information; further information rarely provided on request.

(1) Responses often lack necessary information; further information rarely provided.

(0) Unable to respond to the audience.

Total Rubric Points: _____ × Weight Factor _____ = _____

Score: _____ / _____ = _____ %

Chapter 7

Integrated Field Trips

As gifted education teachers, we understand that a great deal of creative learning takes place outside of the four classroom walls. Field trips are an essential part of the educational environment. Some excellent educators do not include them in their lesson plans because they feel they are not worth the added effort for the expected results. Nothing can be further from the truth. Properly executed field trips should have the following objectives. They should:

- enhance student ability to integrate scientific, mathematical, social, and cultural curriculum into a real-world environment;
- engage educators in detailed lesson plan development for the use of a specific field trip with their students;
- allow teachers to meet with educators, curators, and staff faculties to discuss how each field trip destination (e.g., museum, interactive learning center) can meet their individual integrated curriculum needs;

- improve the ethnic and cultural opportunities for you and your students;
- help teachers to set up field trips for students and colleagues with minimal amounts of effort;
- provide teachers with the opportunity to learn the specific procedures of taking students outside of the classroom, such as student safety, bus procedures and cost, district/school/parent permission forms, chaperone responsibilities, student discipline and supervision, and lunch arrangements;
- improve students' understanding of the relationship between history, art, math, science, the environment, language, and technology; and
- integrate state standards with field trip activities.

When considering a field trip as part of your curriculum, there are several issues that you should consider. A focused field trip provides students with an experience that:
- corresponds to the current classroom curriculum,
- achieves well-defined learning objectives as related to the state standards,
- engages students in the classroom and at the field trip site using strategies such as problem-based learning,
- utilizes the range of resources developed by the field trip site, including its website and education personnel, and
- portrays various locations as resources for lifelong learning.

There are various types of field trip activities available. These include:
- search and find (scavenger hunts);
- recreate the object (sketching, drawing, field trip scrapbooks);
- categorize objects (labeling activities);
- fact-finding and note-taking (fill-in-the-blank worksheets);
- create a narrative (create your own exhibit, creative writing, explore connections to literature); and
- test a hypothesis/collect evidence (problem-based worksheets).

It is important to use your natural teaching ability to help make your field trip successful:
- Keep your goals modest. Don't try to do too much in a single day.
- Develop a discipline policy (see below).
- Talk to the education department personnel at the desired location for guidance and assistance. They are really good at help-

ing teachers with multiple issues, including customizing trips to meet a classroom's needs.

- Check out the desired destination's website. Websites usually have great resource tools that are very teacher friendly. You often can register for field trips directly online and obtain most of your important information.
- Schedule in a break and know where the restrooms are (trust me on that one).
- Get maps, brochures, and other important information in advance. Many of these items can be found online.
- Factor in time to talk about what you see while at the field trip location. Keep students engaged.
- When planning, it is fine to let personal preference surface. Trust your own judgment.

Prepare for the bus ahead of time and have a discipline policy in place:

- Call the bus company well in advance to obtain an estimated cost. Some field trip locations provide free buses, so be sure to ask if that is offered.
- If your bus needs to be back early, check the local area for another bus company that will fit better with your timeline— not theirs. Do not let the bus company dictate your schedule.
- If using multiple buses, assign an equal number of students to each bus. Remind students that there will be no bus-switching allowed.
- Set up written behavior guidelines in advance, and give parents and students a copy. This works extremely well for older students. See Figure 2 for an example of a policy I used with my Ski Club students for 22 years.

It is important to work with your colleagues and obtain "buy-in" from those in charge:

- Share your lesson plan for the field trip with all parties involved. Administrators need to know that your field trip is not a "blow-off" day.
- Discuss your intentions and rationale for taking the field trip with your administrator/department chair prior to going on the trip.
- Get your colleagues involved in the process. Specialists love to help, so ask them to help chaperone.
- If you run into a colleague who is closed-minded about taking field trips, share your entire lesson plan packet and briefly

Cooper Middle School Ski Club Discipline Policy

Due to the nature of the sport and the age of the skier, I demand and expect a high degree of discipline among my young skiers. My highly successful safety record proves this is the only avenue to travel. Very few schools offer the quality of program we have here at Cooper. Therefore, I ask your cooperation in detailing the importance of mature behavior to your child so that this will be as safe and enjoyable season as in the past. Every season, a fair number of warnings, suspensions, and expulsions are handed out.

I strongly advise that if you feel your child cannot or will not follow the prescribed set of rules set forth in this letter that you save your money and *not* join. Our policies will be strictly enforced and all skiers and the parents will be responsible for them. *Please remember that there will be no refunds for suspensions or expulsions due to the Discipline Policy.*

Serious Offenses:
- Skipping a meal or a required ski lesson.
- Swearing/foul language anywhere on the trip.
- Rude behaviors to a chaperone, ski instructor, and/or ski patroller.
- "Hot-dogging" or not skiing in control, including ski jumping.
- Use of any type of drug, including alcohol or tobacco. (Automatic club expulsion/state police called.)

Serious Offense Consequences:
- 1st Offense: 1 trip suspension
- 2nd Offense: Expelled from club

Minor Offenses:
- Any type of immature/loud behavior on the bus that would be considered dangerous/disrupting to any bus passenger. That includes loud talking, not facing forward, and changing seats.
- Parents not picking skier up on time. (If a parent is late picking up a group of skiers, all members get an offense.)
- Not wearing ski club ear sweater on slopes.
- Arriving late for a scheduled bus departure.
- Poor or inappropriate conduct at the lodge or on the slopes.

Minor Offense Consequences:
- 1st Offense: Official warning
- 2nd Offense: 1 trip suspension
- 3rd Offense: Expelled from club

Offenses During Final Trip of Season:
- 6th or 7th grade: Warning/Suspension carried forward to next season.
- 8th grade: After school detentions given.

Your child is representing our Cooper Middle School family and its entire student body. His or her behavior is reflective of your family as well as ours. Your support is appreciated.

Figure 2. Discipline policy example.

explain your objective. If to no avail, oh well—just move on without them!

Do a Pre-Visit to the Field Trip Location
- Explore the location freely. Enjoy!
- Play! We know children construct knowledge through interactive play—so can you.

- Connect the information at the location to one of your classroom themes, units, or standards.
- Be a kid watcher. See how they interact in the institution, and think about your own students.
- Look at the exhibits for their learning potential. What do you see that promotes language development, scientific thinking, problem solving, social development, and cooperative grouping?
- Check out the education department or talk to a coordinator or educator associated with the institution to get further ideas for developing your own field trip.

Finally, when planning your field trip, use the Field Trip Lesson Plan page. Share this completed form with your colleagues and administrators. It works! I have trained thousands of teachers on the art of running comprehensive field trips and their feedback has been tremendous. The key to success in running your own field trip is the implementation of your state educational standards. When you make that initial phone call or visit to the destination you have in mind, ask if its programs are tied to your state standards. If not, go online and check which of your field trip objectives are tied to state standards. If your school district has specific local standards, add those to your write-up. An overview of the field trip process has been provided in Table 1 on page 149.

FIELD TRIP LESSON PLAN

Name _____   Grade Level _____

Destination:

Main Curriculum/Subject Areas:

Topic/Title:

State Standards:

Objective(s) of the Trip:

Pre-Visit Activities:

Field Trip Activities:

Post-Visit Activities:

Table 1
Overview of the Field Trip Process

	Tips for Planning and Administration:	Building on Your Curriculum:	Suggested Activities:	Successful Experience if Students:
Before the Visit	▪ Secure school/district approval for field trip. ▪ Reserve early. ▪ Check the location's website for information. ▪ Ensure compliance with the location's policy. ▪ Call the education department at the location, if applicable. ▪ Work with colleagues during coordination and planning.	▪ Complete Field Trip Lesson Plan page. ▪ Utilize the location's resources as you prepare your lesson.	▪ Familiarize students with the location's environment. ▪ Read literature relevant to field trip themes. ▪ Conduct labs/hands-on activities that correspond to the location. ▪ Review the location's website for possible activities. ▪ Preview online tour of exhibit.	▪ Have realistic expectations about what they will do and see. ▪ Understand how the field trip fits into what they have been studying. ▪ Understand the goals for their learning experience.
During the Visit	▪ Review your confirmation. ▪ Recruit chaperones early from school. ▪ Prepare nametags. ▪ Review rules/discipline. ▪ Provide bus driver with directions and a map to the location. ▪ Develop and follow a check-in process.	▪ Bring props and prepare any relevant artifacts that might fit with the location. ▪ Include both structured and free time.	▪ Provide journaling activities. ▪ Include a mix of small- and large-group activities that correspond to key individual activities.	▪ Are actively engaged. ▪ Are responsive to employees at the location and have fun. ▪ Leave the location with a great understanding of the content/standards presented.
After the Visit	▪ Evaluate experience with location staff, chaperones, and students. ▪ Share feedback with administration.	▪ Link any prior learning with post-visit discussion. ▪ Provide closure for unit and transition to next unit of instruction. ▪ Utilize the location's resources to extend experiments and themes into the classroom.	▪ Provide reflection exercises. ▪ Have students create a story, banner, diorama, or other project about the exhibit. ▪ Use location's website activities. ▪ Assess students' learning based on field trip activities.	▪ Meet all of your learning objectives/state standards. ▪ Make connections between what was learned at the location and what has been taught in the classroom. ▪ View location as a learning resource, and think of it as a fun and exciting place. ▪ Talk to family and friends about their field trip experience.

Chapter 8

Science Holiday Songs

One of your most important duties as a teacher of the gifted is to let the students know you appreciate their hard work and that you like to have a little fun. There is no better time to do that than over the holiday season. I have rewritten several popular holiday songs. This was a great activity to include in my classes on the day before winter vacation. Although my students were of every possible religious and ethnic background, and I have had numerous administrators who would warn public school teachers about religious themes/activities in the classroom, I never had a complaint about this unusual, but electrifying, activity. (I would always have complaints about my singing voice—but that's a whole other story.)

At times, I would allow my students who play musical instruments to bring them to accompany us in the singing. Now, some of the lyrics relate directly to some of the things we did in my specific lab/classroom. But here is an opportunity for you and/or your students to be creative and change them to fit what you do in your classroom. Practice singing the song out loud before you have your students try them—maybe in front of a mirror or some family members. In many places you can substitute various pronouns such as "she" for "he" or place your or a colleague's name in the appropriate places that are underlined and, if music/songwriting is not your greatest talent, don't worry—just have fun with it.

Lab Reports

(as sung to "Jingle Bells")

Dashing through the lab
With a 20-page lab report
Taking all those tests
And laughing at dumb jokes (Ha, Ha, Ha)
Bells for fire drills ring
Making spirits bright
Oh, what fun it is to laugh and sing
A chemistry song tonight.

Oh lab reports, lab reports
Reacting all the way
Oh what fun it is to study
For a chemistry test today.

Chemistry test, thinking test
Isn't it a BLAST?
Oh, what fun it is to take a
Chemistry test and pass. HEY!

Working on group essays
Webs and team reports
Deadly chemicals at a glance
Doing atoms with the neutron dance
Singing the element song
The scientific method isn't wrong
Trying to pass Mr. P's class
Can be a real pain in the _ _ _ (arsenic).

Oh lab reports, lab reports
Reacting all the way
Oh what fun it is to study
For a chemistry test today.

Chemistry test, thinking test
Isn't it a BLAST?
Oh what fun it is to take a
Chemistry test and pass. HEY!

Chemistry Wonderland

(as sung to "Winter Wonderland")

Gases explode are you listening?
In your test tube copper glistens
A beautiful sight our lab is tonight
Walking in a chemistry wonderland.

Chem reactions are a showin'
Chemicals are a flowin'
A beautiful sight our lab is tonight
Walking in a chemistry wonderland.

Gone away is the physical change
As the atoms do not rearrange
A beautiful sight our lab is tonight
Walking in a chemistry wonderland.

In the beaker we make an explosive
And decide if it will blow you up
My lab partner asks, "Is this reaction my friend?"
But does it really MATTER in the end?"

Later on as we calculate
The amount of solid in our nitrate
We'll face unafraid
Precipitate that we made
Walking in a chemistry wonderland.

You can always do a flame test
Your results may not always be the best
Our lab reactions can be real mean
But they will guarantee your brain will be real clean
All the elements are your child
In our lab, you're thrown out if you're wild
A beautiful sight our lab is tonight
Walking in a chemistry wonderland.

Silver Nitrate

(as sung to "Silver Bells")

Silver nitrate, silver nitrate
It's chemistry time in the chem lab
Ding-a-lings, copper rings
Soon it will be chemistry day.

Take your acids, in solution
Add your copper in style
In the beaker there's a feeling of reactions
Silver forming, blue solutions
Bringing ooohs, ahs, and wows
Now the scientific process begins

Get the mass, change to grams
What is the reaction with acid?
Write the equation—balance it
We're glad it's chemistry day.

(Your name), the Wacky Scientist

(as sung to "Rudolph the Red Nose Reindeer")

(Your name), the Wacky Scientist
Had a very goofy class
And if you ever saw him
You would know his labs are a BLAST

All of the others teachers
Used to laugh and call him names
They never let poor (your name)
Join in any atomic games.

Then one foggy scientific night
(Name of principal) came to say,
"(Your name), with your explosions so bright
Won't you guide (name of your school) tonight?"

Then all the teachers loved him
As they shouted out with glee
(Your name), the Wacky Scientist
You'll go down in history—or science.

'Twas the Night Before Chem Test

(as spoken to "'Twas the Night Before Christmas")

'Twas the night before chem test,
The lab was quite still;
Not a burner was burning
Nor had they the will.
The test tubes were placed
in their racks with great care
In hopes that (your name)
Soon would be there.

The students were sleeping
So sound in their room,
All dreaming of explosions,
And hoping no doom.
(Name of colleague) in his apron
(Name of colleague) in his smock
Were sitting, recovering
From semester end shock.

When outside the lab
There rose such a roar.
We leaped from our lab stool—
And fell flat on the floor.
Out to the fire exit
All of us flew.
What was the commotion?
Not one of us knew.

The lights were turned on
The lab was so bright
What we saw next,
Oh what a fright!
My fume-blinded eyes
Then viewed dare I say
Eight charged particles pulling
A chemistry sleigh.

And holding chemical bonds
Students said, "Oh, gee!"
Was a figure I knew
As our own (your name).
With speeds in excess
Of most X-rays they came
As they sped along
He called each one by name.

Now oxygen, now hydrogen,
Now iron and gold
On carbon, on sulfur,
How could you be so bold?
Forget what you know
Of that randomness stuff,
Let's go straight to the roof,
If you've had quanta enough.

As fluids start flowing,
They vibrate with a pinch
"Those tests," said (name of colleague),
"They are really a cinch."
So up to the lab roof
(name of colleague) she did sped
With (your name) safe,
In his chemistry shed.

Just a microsecond later
Many explosions they showed
Charged particles were coming
To our lab abode.
We raced back inside,
And what do you think?
Down the fume hood (your name) fell—
Right into the sink!

He was dressed in a lab coat
Quite ragged and old,
With removable buttons
The "in" style, we're told.
A tray full of beakers
He clutched to this heart,
And under his arm,
A periodic chart.
His eyes through our goggles,
I just couldn't see,
His hands were all yellow
From H-N-0-3.
His face looked quite shocking,
With his hair all around
Like a lab test for copper,
That same shade of brown.

We saw flames and fire
But (your name) was having a ball
I know he was there just
Right down the hall.
The smoke billowed forth
From his angular face,
And with particle movement
Covered the entire place.

He was thin as a match
And not terribly tall,
He wasn't the type
I'd expect at all.
But look at his clothes,
In our lab's harsh white light,
With their acid-burn holes
He's a chemist all right.

He didn't say much
He had no time to kill,
And filled all the test tubes
With barely a spill.
Then placing them back
On the counters with care,
He dashed to the fume hood
And rose through the air.

He called to his students
As they all took off,
Study with care,
From our element trough.
As he flew down the street,
"Good luck on your chem test,
And may your lab stations stay neat."

The 12 Days of Science

(as sung to "The 12 Day of Christmas")

On the 12th day of science
(Your name) gave to me:
Twelve big explosions,
Eleven molecules,
Ten-page test,
Nine grams of chemicals,
Eight lab record book pages,
Seven unknown samples,
Six flaming test tubes,
Five golden beakers.
Four dissected frogs,
Three-D periodic tables,
Two Bunsen burners,
And a science fair project for (your name).

Silent Labs

(as sung to "Silent Night")

Silent labs, difficult labs
All with math, all with graphs.
That spills nitric acid we see it fell,
Data processing, results are real swell.
And my conclusions came very fast,
Oh how long will science class last?

I'm Dreaming of a White Precipitate

(as sung to "I'm Dreaming of a White Christmas")

I'm dreaming of a white precipitate
Just like the ones I used to know.
Where the colors are vivid and (your name) is livid
To see impurities in the snow.
I'm dreaming of a white precipitate
With every chemistry test I write.
May your equations be balanced and
right—and may all your reactions be bright!

(Your Name) Is Comin' to Town

(as sung to "Santa Claus Is Comin' to Town")

You better not weight,
You better not mass,
You better not react,
Or you get kicked out of class,
(Your name) is coming to town.

He's balancing an equation,
He's checking it twice,
He's goin' to find out
The heat of melting ice,
(Your name) is coming to town.

He sees you when you're working,
He knows the chemicals you take
He knows when you are safe or not,
So wear goggles for goodness sake.

Oh, you better clean up your lab,
Or pay a large lab fee,
You better study hard,
To pass chemistry you see
(Your name) is coming to town.

About the Author

Phil Parratore has been an advocate of hands-on science for gifted students for more than three decades. He has a real passion for getting children and adults involved with science education. His philosophy is very simple: Gifted children learn best by active participation in the understanding of abstract concepts.

As a retired middle school math and science teacher for regular education, as well as gifted education students, Phil has served as a science consultant to numerous school districts throughout the United States. Phil holds a master's degree in school administration and secondary education. At the university graduate level, he has trained more than 5,000 students in the art of hands-on science.